LOVE GAMES: DECODING MODERN ROMANCE

Vidhisha Chaturvedi

INDIA · SINGAPORE · MALAYSIA

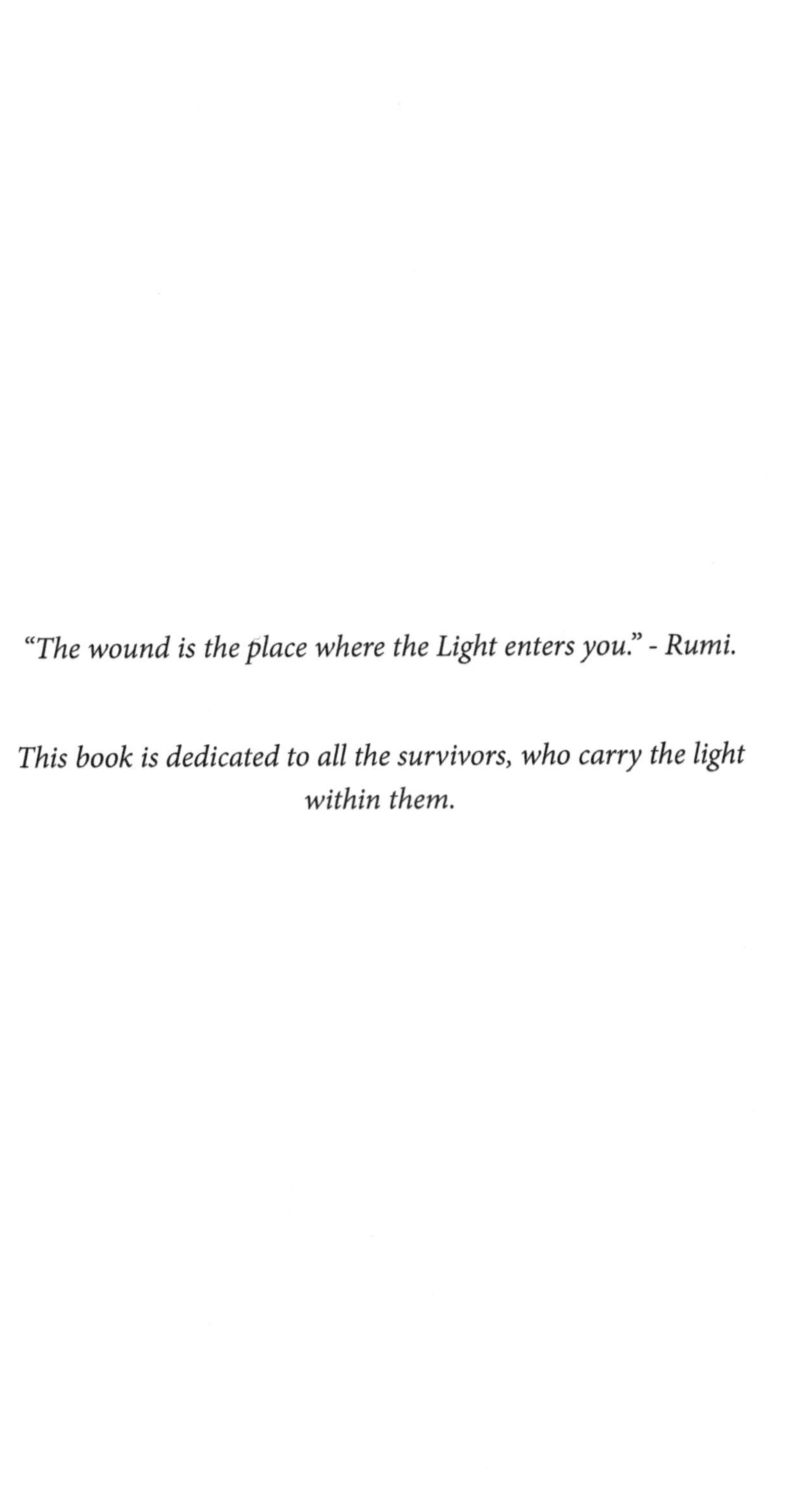

"The wound is the place where the Light enters you." - Rumi.

This book is dedicated to all the survivors, who carry the light within them.

Contents

Contents

Preface

Ah, love. The four-letter word that has captivated poets, philosophers, heartbroken teenagers and adults for millennia. But in the age of swipes and likes, algorithms and endless profiles, the landscape of romance has undergone a dramatic shift. Welcome to the world of modern romance, a complex game where the rules are constantly rewritten and the stakes are your heart.

This book is your guide to navigating the sometimes-treacherous, often-hilarious, and undeniably exhilarating world of modern dating. We'll delve into the rise of technology and its impact on finding love, exploring how dating apps have become the new matchmakers, while simultaneously creating a culture of back benching and curated online personas.

But fear not, fellow love seekers! We'll also unpack the secrets to success in the digital age. From crafting a profile that truly reflects you to navigating the delicate dance of online conversations, we'll equip you with the tools to decipher the signals (and red flags) of modern romance.

Beyond the digital realm, we'll explore the evolution of love itself. How have changing gender roles and societal expectations impacted what we seek in a partner? What does it mean to find a fulfilling and lasting connection in a world obsessed with instant gratification?

This isn't just a book about finding "the one" (although, if that's your goal, we've got you covered!). It's about understanding your own desires, embracing your authentic self, and creating a love story that's uniquely yours. So, put on your metaphorical dancing shoes, grab a glass of courage, and get ready to decode the love games of the modern world. It's time to rewrite the rules and find a love that's as genuine and thrilling as it is real.

Acknowledgement

To all those who journeyed with me through the tumultuous terrain of Love Games - Decoding Modern Romance, I extend my heartfelt "thank you." My deepest gratitude goes to the brave souls who connected with me over a story shared on the Humans of Bombay page which sparked conversations that illuminated the complexities of relationships in the digital age. From the depths of heartbreak to the highs of genuine connection, your experiences became the canvas upon which this book was painted.

Thank you to the teachers of tough love. Those who unintentionally (or perhaps intentionally) challenged my heart – your actions, though painful, fueled my resilience and self-discovery.

This book is a testament to the human spirit's capacity to endure, to learn, and to love again despite the scars of past wounds. It is a tribute to the courage it takes to navigate the minefield of modern dating and emerge stronger on the other side.

This isn't just my story, it's ours. To everyone who engaged in heartfelt conversations, shared observations, or simply witnessed the evolution of love in the digital age – thank you. From handwritten letters to instant messages, this book reflects the collective journey we've taken as human connection adapts to a new era.

With heartfelt appreciation, Vidhisha

Introduction

Forget fairytales, this is cuffing season in the digital age! Welcome to Love Games: Decoding Modern Romance, your guide to navigating the wild world of swiping right, Netflix nights, and the ever-evolving landscape of love.

Imagine scrolling through endless profiles on Tinder or Bumble, each face a potential happily-ever-after (or a hilarious horror story for your next brunch date). Love in the 21st century is a whirlwind of confusing texts (is that single eggplant emoji a compliment or a red flag?), curated Instagram feeds portraying picture-perfect relationships (never mind the fights happening off-camera), and the pressure to find "the one" fueled by reality shows like "Love Is Blind" and "The Bachelor" (because falling in love in a pod or a rose ceremony is totally realistic, right?).

This book is your backstage pass to the enthralling drama of modern relationships. We'll delve into the complex mix of technology, social shifts, and changing mindsets that have transformed dating into a thrilling yet perplexing maze. From the exhilarating rush of a "match" notification to the soul-crushing silence of being ghosted, each chapter peels back the layers of today's love life, offering juicy insights, eye-opening revelations, and cautionary tales to help you navigate the game.

Think of this book as your wingman (or wingwoman) – we'll equip you with the knowledge to decipher cryptic dating app messages, the confidence to navigate the murky waters of situationships, and the wisdom to avoid falling for the carefully crafted online personas that often mask reality. We'll explore the ever-changing dynamics of texting, where a simple "hey" can spark endless possibilities or leave you hanging for days. We'll analyse the phenomenon of "sliding into DMs," a modern courtship ritual governed by emojis, memes, and carefully crafted opening lines.

Get ready for a wild ride through the twists and turns of love in the digital age. This book is your key to mastering the rules, cracking the codes, and finding your own happily-ever-after, whatever that may look like for you in this crazy world of love.

Chapter 1

Attraction and Connection - The Foundation of Modern Romance

Welcome, love navigators, to the exhilarating first chapter of "Love Games – Decoding Modern Romance!" Buckle up as we dive into the emoji-fueled world of attraction and connection, the foundation of every epic love story (or hilarious first-date disaster!).

Consider this chapter your treasure map to understanding the irresistible forces that draw us together – the initial spark and the flame that keeps the connection burning bright.

From Swipes to Soulmates: A Love Story in the Digital Age

The aroma of freshly brewed coffee mingled with the clatter of mugs and lively chatter in the bustling Italian cafe. Sarah perched on a stool, scrolled through endless profiles on her phone. Disappointment gnawed at her – curated selfies, generic bios boasting about "wanderlust," and a stifling sense of everyone playing the same game.

Suddenly, a notification popped up. Unlike the usual text messages, it was an audio message. Intrigued, Sarah pressed play.

A chuckle, followed by a self-deprecating joke about navigating the awkward "what do you do?" stage on a first date, filled her ears. It was refreshingly genuine.

Curious, she opened his profile. Ethan's photo wasn't the typical gym selfie, but a candid shot of him volunteering at a local community garden, helping kids plant vibrant wildflowers. His bio, a delightful mix of witty observations and indie music references, felt instantly relatable.

The bustling cafe faded away. Sarah found herself smiling, sending an audio message back – a playful jab about his taste in music (he was a die-hard Mumford & Sons fan, much to her amusement). They messaged for hours, not about careers or travel destinations, but about their passions – Ethan's fascination with lesser-known local history, Sarah's secret love for quirky stand-up comedy routines.

Days turned into a week, filled with voice notes that stretched into the night, shared Spotify playlists featuring a mix of classic rock and up-and-coming artists, and playful debates about the merits of adding sprinkles to donuts (Ethan, surprisingly, was a fan). There was a spark, undeniable, fueled by shared humour and a genuine connection that went beyond the screen.

Finally, the day arrived for their date. Sarah, usually a master of first-date composure, felt a flutter of nerves. Ethan, however, was exactly as his profile portrayed – charmingly awkward, with a smile that could rival the summer sun.

They didn't follow the script. Instead, comfortable conversation flowed, referencing their late-night voice messages and inside jokes. They wandered through the bustling farmer's market, a sensory overload of colourful produce, fragrant flowers, and the rhythmic calls of vendors. Ethan, captivated by a hand-carved wooden birdhouse, shared a fascinating story about the local craftsman who made them, his enthusiasm disarming Sarah's usual cynicism.

Later, at a cosy bistro, they devoured creamy bowls of pasta, debating the merits of pesto versus bolognese. Hours flew by, a comfortable silence punctuated by bursts of laughter and shared stories.

As the night ended, a hesitant goodbye hung in the air. Then, Ethan surprised her, his voice dropping to a soft murmur. "This was... incredible. Would you like to, maybe, catch that new documentary about the Elephant Whisperers everyone's talking about?"

Sarah's heart skipped a beat. "With coffee and pastries, of course?"

Ethan grinned, his eyes twinkling. "Absolutely not. But I'm open to negotiation."

And as they walked away, fingers brushing, Sarah realised that in the age of swiping, she'd found something rare – a connection built on shared passions, genuine humour, and the magic of a voice that resonated with her soul. It wasn't just attraction, it was the promise of something deeper, a connection forged in the digital age but blossoming in the real world, one quirky message and shared laugh at a time.

The following week unfolded like a scene from a classic romantic comedy. Ethan, ever the charmer, surprised Sarah with a handwritten note tucked into her favourite coffee order – a playful poem referencing their donut debate. Sarah, never one to shy away from a challenge, retaliated with a strategically placed box of her favourite cupcakes at his office reception, accompanied by a teasing voicemail threatening dire consequences if he didn't accept her "peace offering."

Their weekend date was a whirlwind adventure. They explored a historic local landmark, Ethan regaling her with tales of revolutionaries and battles that came alive amidst the weathered stone walls. Later, under a sky ablaze with a million stars, they shared childhood dreams and whispered secrets, the crackling bonfire casting a warm glow on their faces.

As days turned into weeks, their connection deepened. Sarah discovered a hidden tenderness in Ethan, a man who could quote Shakespeare with the same ease he discussed the merits of a perfectly brewed cup of coffee. Ethan, in turn, was captivated by Sarah's sharp wit and her infectious laughter that echoed through their late-night phone calls.

One rainy afternoon, huddled under a shared umbrella, their conversation took a serious turn. They spoke about their hopes and fears for the future, their dreams intertwining like the threads of a vibrant quilt. Ethan confessed his desire to open a local history walking tour company. Sarah, an aspiring environmental engineer, shared her dream of designing sustainable housing projects that blended modern technology with historic preservation.

In each other's eyes, they saw not just a partner, but a cheerleader, a confidante, a home. There were challenges, of course. Ethan's family, steeped in tradition, was initially hesitant about his unconventional career change. Sarah, fiercely independent, grappled with the idea of relying on someone else.

But their connection, nurtured in the fertile ground of shared passions and genuine understanding, held strong. They tackled each hurdle together, Sarah's unwavering support bolstering Ethan's confidence, and Ethan's grounded perspective providing a balance for Sarah's ambitious dreams.

Years later, their love story had become a local legend. They built a life together, a tapestry woven with threads of tradition and innovation. On weekends, they conducted history walking tours together, their voices weaving tales of the past for the eager tourists. Ethan's passion for local history was infectious, and Sarah's knowledge of sustainable practices often found its way into their tours, highlighting the importance of preserving the past while building for the future.

In the evenings, they sat on their porch swing, sipping tea and watching the sunset paint the sky in hues of orange and pink. Their laughter echoed through the quiet neighbourhood, a testament to the enduring power of a connection that blossomed in the age of swiping, a love story born from a voice message and a shared love for donuts, sprinkles or not.

One blustery autumn afternoon, as they sorted through a box of old keepsakes, Sarah stumbled upon a worn cassette tape. A smile bloomed on her face as she recognised Ethan's handwriting on the label: "Our First Laugh - Don't Forget the Raisins!" They popped the tape into a dusty player, and the familiar sound of Ethan's voice filled the room, his self-deprecating joke about surviving the first-date gauntlet sparking another round of laughter. The years melted away, and for a moment, they were back in the bustling cafe, two souls finding connection in a digital world, a connection that had blossomed into a love story that would forever be etched in their hearts, a reminder of the magic that could unfold with just a single voice message and a shared spark.

The Allure of Attraction

Attraction is the electric jolt that ignites it all. It's that butterflies-in-your-stomach feeling you get when you spot someone intriguing across a crowded room (remember those?), or, more likely these days, across your phone screen while swiping through endless dating profiles. But what makes us swipe right or feel that undeniable pull towards someone?

Attraction in the Digital Age:

The Late-Night Text Marathon: The clock ticks past midnight, yet the notifications keep buzzing. A witty banter flows between two screens, fueled by a shared sense of humour and a growing curiosity. Sleep can wait, replaced by the intoxicating thrill of a budding connection.

The Unexpected Swipe Right: A face pops up on the dating app, different from the usual types. A quirky bio or an intriguing photo sparks an unexpected interest. A right swipe, a chance taken, a seed of attraction planted in the digital soil.

The Voice Note Surprise: After weeks of texting, a voice note arrives. The sound of their laugh, the warmth in their tone, adds a new dimension to the attraction. Texting can't capture the nuances that ignite a spark, a feeling that goes beyond the screen.

The Shared Playlist: A Spotify playlist lands in your inbox, a carefully curated selection of songs. Each track whispers a secret, revealing a shared taste in music, a vulnerability that fuels the attraction. Suddenly, you hear the world through their ears, a connection blossoming through melody.

Connection Beyond the App

The Coffee Shop "Bump-In": Planned dates are great, but fate has a way of intervening. A chance encounter at a familiar coffee shop leads to a stolen conversation, a connection that transcends the virtual world. Suddenly, the online persona becomes a real person, and the spark intensifies.

The Comfortable Silence: Words aren't always necessary. Sitting together, lost in a book or simply basking in comfortable silence, speaks volumes. A shared sense of ease, a feeling of being understood without explanation, cements the connection beyond the initial spark.

The Late-Night Heart-to-Heart: Hours melt away as vulnerabilities are shared, dreams are confided, and fears are confessed. Under the cloak of darkness, a deeper connection forms, built on trust and a willingness to be truly seen.

The Supportive Text After a Tough Day: A bad day at work, a fight with a friend, a life hurdle overcome – a perfectly timed text arrives, offering support and understanding. This simple gesture shows they care, solidifying the connection and reminding you that you're not alone.

Science of Desire

Physical Chemistry: It all starts with physical appearance, often the initial trigger for attraction. Evolutionary psychologist Dr. David Buss suggests that symmetry, body language, and other visual cues signal health and vitality, which are subconscious indicators of genetic fitness. But remember, beauty truly lies in the eye of the beholder, shaped by personal preferences and ever-evolving cultural norms.

Beyond the Surface: While physical attraction is the initial spark, emotional and intellectual connections are the glue that keep the flames alive. Shared values, a good sense of humour, empathy, and intellectual stimulation create deeper, more lasting bonds. As Dr. Helen Fisher puts it, *"Love is more than just physical attraction. The brain plays a crucial role, and it's the chemistry of our personalities that truly matters."*

The Power of Duality: Birds of a Feather? Similarity creates a sense of comfort and understanding. We often vibe with those who share our interests and passions. But don't underestimate the allure of opposites! The classic case of "opposites attract" highlights how complementary personalities can bring a dynamic and enriching dimension to a relationship.

Building the Bridge - From Spark to Connection: Attraction ignites the initial spark, but a strong connection is what fans the flames and keeps the fire burning. Building a meaningful connection takes time, effort, and a willingness to invest in each other.

Real Connections in a Digital World: Imagine Olivia and Harper meeting through a book club app. Despite living in different cities, they build a deep bond through consistent communication, sharing personal stories and dreams. Video calls, virtual book discussions, and the occasional weekend visit solidify their connection, proving that shared passions and consistent communication can bridge geographical distances.

Friendship First: Let's not forget the power of friendship as a foundation for love. Take Nova and Jasper - childhood friends, neighbours, colleagues and best friends for years before romance blossomed. Their shared history, unwavering support, and deep understanding of each other's backgrounds, likes and dislikes, and quirks laid a solid foundation for a lasting love story.

The Essential Ingredients

Open Communication: Honest and open communication is the cornerstone of any strong relationship. Sharing thoughts, feelings, and experiences builds trust and understanding. Active listening and empathy ensure both partners feel heard and valued. Remember, as William Paisley said, *"Communication is the fuel that keeps the fire of your relationship burning."*

Building Trust: Trust is the bedrock of a healthy connection. It's built over time through consistent behaviour, reliability, and honesty. Trust allows for vulnerability and intimacy, enabling partners to be their authentic selves without fear. Stephen Covey perfectly captures this sentiment: *"Trust is the glue of life. It's the most essential ingredient in effective communication. It's the foundational principle that holds all relationships."*

The Treasure of Lasting Love

Attraction and connection, the irresistible forces we explored in this chapter, are like the compass and map guiding us on the journey of love. Attraction ignites the initial spark, while connection fans the flame and keeps it burning bright.

Understanding the science behind attraction and the elements that build connection equips you to navigate the exciting, and sometimes bewildering, world of modern romance. Remember, a fulfilling relationship thrives on nurturing both aspects. Cultivate physical and emotional intimacy, prioritise open communication, and invest in shared experiences to create a foundation of trust and understanding.

As you embark on your own love adventures, keep this treasure map close. With a healthy dose of self-awareness and a commitment to fostering both attraction and connection, you'll be well on your way to discovering the true treasure – a lasting and meaningful partnership.

Chapter 2

The Honey Trap - Sweet Deception in Modern Romance

Welcome, love adventurers, to a chapter that delves into the darker side of modern romance: the honey trap. Here, we'll explore the manipulative tactics employed by those who lure unsuspecting hearts into deceptive relationships for personal gain.

Tokyo Twilight: Love and Deception in the Neon Jungle

In the neon-drenched jungle of Tokyo, where secrets pulsed beneath the glittering facade, a story unfolded that would forever alter the destinies of Maya, a tenacious investigative journalist, and Kai, a captivating enigma shrouded in mystery.

Maya, with a nose for trouble and a heart yearning for truth, found herself embedded in the shadowy realm of yakuza infiltration. Tasked with exposing the insidious web of honeypots – women deployed to seduce and manipulate powerful figures – she fixated on the elusive mastermind codenamed Kitsune, the Fox. Enthralled by the whispered rumours of his guile and the thrill of the forbidden, Maya embarked on a dangerous quest to unveil the truth.

Meanwhile, Kai, a man sculpted by moonlight and secrets, navigated a life of duality. Under the harsh glare of the day, he commanded respect as the heir to a vast technological empire. But as the city surrendered to the velvet cloak of night, he donned the mantle of Kitsune, a master manipulator who orchestrated elaborate honeypot schemes. His targets: influential politicians and corporate titans, ensnared by the charm and empty promises offered by his carefully chosen operatives.

Fate, a mischievous deity in the neon jungle, orchestrated a chance encounter between Maya and Kai at a high-stakes gala. Across the glittering expanse of the ballroom, their eyes met, igniting a spark that crackled with forbidden electricity. Maya, captivated by Kai's enigmatic aura, felt a thrill course through her. Kai, in turn, was drawn to Maya's unwavering spirit and the glint of investigative fire in her eyes.

As stolen moments blossomed into clandestine rendezvous, Kai wove a tapestry of illusion, blurring the lines between reality and desire. He painted a picture of a life filled with adrenaline-fueled adventures and a future steeped in luxury – a world that resonated with Maya's yearning for escape. Blinded by the intoxicating facade, Maya surrendered to the whirlwind romance, oblivious to the truth lurking beneath the surface.

Unease, a persistent shadow, began to gnaw at Maya's heart. Whispers of Kai's past, laced with rumours of broken hearts and shattered lives, reached her ears. Torn between the intoxicating passion and the nagging suspicion, Maya's journalistic instincts roared to life. Fueled by a desperate need for answers, she embarked on a clandestine investigation, venturing deep into Kai's meticulously constructed world.

With each thread she unravelled, a disturbing truth emerged. A trail of heartbroken women, discarded like pawns in a twisted game, led Maya to the undeniable conclusion – Kai, the man she loved, was Kitsune, the mastermind she sought to expose.

Confronted with the weight of her discovery, Maya braced herself for the shattering of illusions. The charming facade crumbled, revealing the calculating predator beneath. A tense stand-off ensued, a battle fueled by betrayal, deceit, and the remnants of a love built on a foundation of lies.

In a heart-stopping climax, Maya, armed with irrefutable evidence, unveiled Kai's elaborate honeypot operation to the world. The city watched, aghast, as the once-untouchable Kitsune's world crumbled. The captivating enigma was finally brought to his knees, his empire reduced to ashes.

And so, Maya's exposé became a stark warning etched in neon against the Tokyo skyline. It served as a chilling reminder that in the age of manufactured realities and fleeting connections, love could be a weapon as potent as deception, a cautionary tale where the line between seduction and manipulation blurred into a dangerous oblivion.

The Art of the Deception

Honey trapping thrives on the allure of charm and false promises. Perpetrators, often adept at reading people, use seduction to build trust and exploit vulnerabilities. This deceptive web can take many forms, from emotional manipulation in personal relationships to financial fraud or even espionage. At its core, honey trapping preys on the emotional desires of the target, ultimately leading them into a situation that can be difficult to escape.

Examples

Catfishing: A fake online dating profile is created using stolen photos and a fabricated persona. The catfish then builds a romantic connection with the target, often showering them with compliments and affection. Eventually, the catfish might make financial requests or exploit the emotional attachment for personal gain.

Emotional Blackmail: Someone might enter a genuine relationship but use it to manipulate the partner. They could threaten to expose sensitive information shared confidentially or use emotional tactics to guilt the partner into giving them money, gifts, or special favours.

Love Bombing: This tactic involves overwhelming the target with excessive affection and attention early on in the relationship. The love bomber might constantly text, call, and shower the target with gifts, creating an illusion of an intense and fast-moving connection. This creates a strong emotional attachment that the honey trapper can then exploit for their benefit.

Fake Break-Up Manipulation: The honey trapper might initiate a fake break-up to test the target's devotion and extract concessions. They might promise to get back together if the target agrees to certain demands, like giving them money or changing their behaviour in a way that benefits the honey trapper.

Feigning Vulnerability: Someone might pretend to be more vulnerable than they are, sharing personal stories or fabricated sob stories to gain sympathy and trust from the target. This emotional manipulation can make the target more susceptible to the honey trapper's requests or exploitation.

Let's dissect some scenarios to understand the honey trap in action:

The Gold Digger: Brian, a successful businessman, falls victim to Veronica's charm. Initially, she seems genuinely interested, fostering a connection that Brian believes is real. However, her true motives surface when she starts pressuring him for extravagant gifts and financial support. By the time Brian realises he's being used, he faces not only financial ruin but also emotional devastation. This scenario mirrors a high-profile case where a businessman was duped by a woman he met at a social event. After gaining his trust, she began requesting loans and expensive jewellery, leaving him financially and reputationally drained.

The Digital Disguise: Aidan, an optimistic young man, believes he's found his perfect match on Bumble. Daily messages and shared secrets create a strong emotional bond. However, when they finally arrange to meet, Aidan discovers a harsh reality: the woman he fell for is a catfish, a fictional persona created to manipulate him. This story reflects the growing phenomenon of online deception, showcased in documentaries like "The Tinder Swindler" on Netflix. Here, individuals create elaborate fake identities to lure unsuspecting victims, often extracting money through fabricated emergencies.

The Hidden Threat: A high-profile UK politician was lured into an affair by a seductive stranger. Unbeknownst to him, the encounters were secretly recorded. This compromising footage became a tool for blackmail, forcing the politician to comply with the perpetrator's demands. The secret recordings of his affair were leaked, leading to public humiliation, career ruin, and personal consequences.

The Deceptive Mind

The honey trapper's psyche often harbours narcissistic or sociopathic tendencies. They excel at manipulation, possessing an uncanny ability to identify and exploit vulnerabilities. Honey trappers can be incredibly charming and persuasive, masking their true intentions with a facade of empathy. They crave control and the thrill of deception, viewing their victims as pawns in a twisted game.

Motivations Unveiled

The reasons behind honey trapping can vary significantly. Some perpetrators are driven by pure greed, using their charm to extract money or financial support from their victims. Others may engage in honey trapping for espionage purposes, gathering sensitive information for personal gain. There are even cases where the motivation is purely psychological, with the perpetrator deriving pleasure from the power and control they exert over their unsuspecting targets.

Guarding Your Heart: Recognising the Red Flags

Being aware of the red flags associated with honey trapping is crucial to safeguarding yourself:

1. **Too Good to Be True:** If someone seems to embody your ideal partner perfectly, it might be a red flag. Honey trappers often

create idealised personas to establish trust and emotional connection rapidly.

2. **Rushed Intimacy:** Be wary of individuals who push for a fast-paced relationship, whether it's emotional intimacy or physical engagement. This urgency could be a tactic to entangle you before you notice inconsistencies.

3. **Inconsistent Stories:** Pay close attention to inconsistencies in their background or personal details. Honey trappers can make mistakes, and their fabricated stories might not always add up.

4. **Excessive Flattery and Attention:** While compliments can be part of genuine affection, an excessive amount of flattery can be a manipulative tool used to lower your guard.

5. **Financial Requests:** Be cautious if someone you've recently met starts asking for money or financial assistance. Genuine relationships rarely involve early financial dependence.

Protecting Yourself in the Digital Age

With the rise of online dating, here are some essential steps to take:

1. **Verify Their Identity:** Use video calls to confirm they are who they say they are, and cross-check their information on social media platforms.

2. **Take Your Time:** Building a relationship takes time. Get to know the person gradually, and be wary of anyone who tries to rush the process.

3. **Maintain Boundaries:** Keep personal information private until you feel confident in their intentions. Don't share details like your financial status or home address too early.

4. **Trust Your Instincts:** If something feels off, it probably is. Listen to your gut feelings and don't ignore red flags, no matter how minor they may seem.

5. **Seek Advice:** Talk to trusted friends or family members about your new relationship. They can offer objective perspectives and may notice red flags that you might miss.

Empowering Yourself: Beyond Protection

While safeguarding yourself is essential, let's not lose sight of the potential beauty of love. Here's how to cultivate a more fulfilling experience:

Embrace Vulnerability: Vulnerability is not weakness; it's a sign of courage. By sharing your authentic self, you attract genuine connections built on trust and understanding.

Seek Authentic Connections: Focus on building relationships based on shared values, mutual respect, and genuine interest. Don't settle for flattery or rushed intimacy.

Communicate Openly: Honest and open communication is the lifeblood of healthy relationships. Express your needs, desires, and concerns openly, and encourage your partner to do the same.

Conclusion: A Brighter Chapter

Honey trapping exposes the dark underbelly of modern romance. However, by understanding these deceptive tactics and prioritising healthy scepticism, we can navigate the landscape of love with greater confidence. Remember, genuine connections flourish through shared experiences and mutual respect, not hurried intimacy or excessive flattery.

Embrace vulnerability, cultivate genuine connections, and prioritise open communication. By fostering these qualities, you rewrite the narrative of honey trapping, transforming it from a story of deception into a celebration of true love. So, love adventurers, embark on your journey with open hearts and clear minds. Remember, the greatest treasures are not found in material gain or fleeting flattery, but in the depths of genuine connection.

Chapter 3

Love Bombing - The Blitzkrieg of Affection

Following the deceptive allure of honey trapping, we delve into another manipulative tactic lurking in the landscape of modern romance: "love bombing." This chapter dismantles the phenomenon of love bombing, where an overwhelming onslaught of affection and attention is deployed to control and manipulate. We'll explore the psychology behind love bombers, their motivations, real-life examples, and equip you with insights to recognise and shield yourself from this insidious strategy.

From Spark to Suffocation: A Love Bombing Story

The first text from Liam buzzed in Amelia's pocket ten minutes after she'd scribbled her number on a napkin and handed it to him across chilled mugs of beer. "Hey, beautiful! I'm so glad I finally got your number. I've been thinking about you all day."

A warmth bloomed in Amelia's chest. He had a way with words, Liam did, and his eyes seemed to hold a universe of unspoken affection. It wasn't every day you met someone who could weave such a spell in the space of a single pub date, amidst the clatter of glasses and the intoxicating smell of freshly brewed beer. Before she knew it, she'd found herself saying yes to dinner, a giddy excitement bubbling in her stomach.

The next few weeks were crazy. Amelia's phone buzzed incessantly with Liam's messages, each one a sweet serenade peppered with endearing emojis. Pre-dawn calls became a routine, his voice a husky whisper promising a future where she was the star and he, her devoted admirer. Flowers, meticulously chosen in her favourite colours, appeared on her doorstep like magic. He showered her with compliments, painting vivid pictures of a perfect life with her by his side. "You're the most stunning woman I've ever met," he'd murmur, his gaze lingering on her a beat too long. "I've never connected with anyone like I connect with you."

Amelia was smitten. He made her feel like a masterpiece, a work of art he couldn't wait to frame and hang in his personal gallery. Every insecurity she harboured seemed to vanish under the warmth of his attention. He was everything she'd ever dreamed of, or at least, that's what she desperately clung to.

But the honeymoon phase, as Liam called it, was fleeting. The constant barrage of texts tapered off, replaced by a deafening silence that stretched for hours. The phone calls became a distant memory, replaced by impersonal voicemails that left Amelia feeling increasingly uneasy. The compliments, once overflowing, now dripped with a subtle condescension. A casual remark about her outfit was met with a furrowed brow and a pointed, "Don't you think something else would be more flattering?"

One evening, after a particularly curt text criticising her choice of restaurant, a knot of unease tightened in Amelia's stomach. She couldn't ignore the shift anymore. "Liam, you've been distant lately," she ventured, her voice barely a whisper. "What's wrong?"

He sighed, a flicker of annoyance crossing his handsome features. "Amelia, you're being too sensitive. It's just a text. Lighten up, would you? I'm just trying to be honest."

Honest? This wasn't honesty. This was a stark contrast to the man who had pursued her with such relentless intensity. The constant praise, the extravagant gifts, the declarations of undying love – it all felt like a distant dream.

Amelia tried to cling to the embers of the love she thought she had, but the cracks were widening with each passing day. His criticisms became a relentless assault, chipping away at her confidence like a sculptor with a cold chisel. He started dissecting her friendships, her career choices, even her family, painting them all in a negative light. It was relentless, a constant barrage of negativity that slowly wore her down.

She soon realised the initial love bomb wasn't love at all. It was a meticulously crafted facade, a calculated manipulation to lure her in and then control her.

Leaving Liam was the hardest thing she'd ever done, her heart a shattered kaleidoscope of emotions. But with each step away, a sliver of her strength returned. Amelia realised that love bombing wasn't love at all. It was a weapon, a way to exploit someone's vulnerabilities.

It took time to heal, to rebuild the shattered pieces of herself. Amelia learned to recognise the red flags, to value her self-worth, and to trust her gut instinct. It was a slow, arduous journey, but one that emerged her stronger, wiser, and ready to love again. But this time, she wouldn't settle for an illusion. She would choose someone who loved the real Amelia.

The Overwhelming Onslaught

Love bombing involves showering someone with excessive attention, admiration, and affection, all with the manipulative goal of gaining control. This initial flood of positive reinforcement can be intoxicating, making the recipient feel extraordinarily valued and special. However, beneath the surface lies a darker agenda – to create a sense of emotional dependence and control.

Examples

The Ensnaring Soulmate: A young female professional, was captivated by a charming man she met on Bumble. From their first encounter, he bombarded her with grand gestures – extravagant gifts, constant texts, and public declarations of love. He swiftly spoke of their future together, claiming she was his soulmate. Initially flattered, the woman found herself drawn into the relationship. However, as the man's intense affection morphed into possessiveness and control, she realised she was trapped in a cycle of manipulation and emotional abuse.

The Cult's Allure: Former members of a cult recounted how their leader used love bombing to recruit and retain followers. Newcomers were welcomed with overwhelming positivity, praise, and promises of a utopian future. This intense initial affection fostered a sense of belonging and loyalty. However, over time, the leader's true intentions emerged, revealing a desire for control and exploitation, leaving members struggling to escape the toxic environment. Documentaries like Netflix's "Wild Wild Country" showcase similar tactics, where charismatic leaders exploit love bombing to create a facade of community and belonging.

The Deceptive Mind of a Love Bomber

The Psyche Love bombers often exhibit traits of narcissism or borderline personality disorder. They crave admiration and control, wielding affection as a weapon to dominate their target. The intense initial attention creates an emotional high, making the target dependent on their validation. Once hooked, the love bomber reveals their manipulative tendencies, often alternating between affection and criticism to maintain control.

The Motivation The motivations behind love bombing can vary. Some love bombers seek to establish control over their victims for personal gratification, using them to boost their own ego. Others may be driven by a desire for power within a relationship or group, aiming to isolate their target from other influences. In some cases, love bombing can be a tool for financial exploitation, similar to honey trapping, where the ultimate goal is to gain access to the target's resources.

Recognising Love Bombing: Red Flags

1. **Excessive Attention:** An overwhelming amount of attention and affection early in the relationship, disproportionate to the time you've known each other.

2. **Rapid Progression:** Attempts to fast-track the relationship, with declarations of love, future plans, and pressure to make significant commitments quickly.

3. **Isolation Tactics:** Subtle or overt efforts to distance you from friends, family, and other support systems, increasing your dependency on the love bomber.

4. **Emotional Rollercoaster:** Shifts between intense affection and sudden withdrawal or criticism, creating an unstable emotional environment that leaves you craving their approval.

5. **Overly Idealised Statements:** Descriptions of the relationship as perfect or destined, often accompanied by exaggerated claims about your unique connection.

Protecting Yourself from the Blitzkrieg

Take It Slow: Resist the pressure to rush the relationship. Allow time for it to develop naturally and for true intentions to surface.

Maintain Independence: Keep your social and support networks intact. Ensure you have a life outside the relationship to maintain perspective and balance.

Set Boundaries: Establish and enforce personal boundaries. Healthy relationships respect each partner's individual space and limits.

Trust Your Instincts: Pay attention to any feelings of discomfort or suspicion. If something feels off, it's important to address it rather than dismissing it.

Seek External Perspectives: Talk to trusted friends or family about your relationship. They can offer objective insights and help identify potential red flags.

The Aftermath: Healing from the Blitz

Surviving a love bombing experience can leave deep emotional scars. The initial high followed by manipulation and control can lead to confusion, self-doubt, and a shattered sense of trust. It's crucial to seek support and engage in self-care to rebuild confidence and emotional resilience. Professional counselling can be particularly beneficial in processing the experience and developing strategies to avoid similar situations in the future.

Conclusion: Love's True Battlefield

Love bombing is a potent weapon in the arsenal of manipulative individuals, used to create an illusion of perfect love while concealing darker intentions. Understanding the tactics and motivations behind love bombing empowers you to navigate the complex world of modern romance with greater awareness. By recognising the red flags and maintaining healthy boundaries, you can safeguard your heart and ensure your relationships are built on genuine affection and mutual respect.

As we navigate the labyrinth of love, knowledge and vigilance are our best defences against the deceptive games that can entrap the unsuspecting. Remember, true love is a journey of mutual respect, shared growth, and emotional safety. Don't settle for the fleeting high of a love bomb – hold out for a love that empowers and uplifts you.

"The greatest happiness of life is the conviction that we are loved - loved for ourselves, or rather, loved in spite of ourselves." - Victor Hugo

Chapter 4

Situationship - Navigating the Undefined Relationship

Modern romance takes many twists and turns, and the concept of the situationship is a prime example. Unlike the clear-cut boundaries of committed relationships or casual flings, situationships reside in a grey area – a space where expectations and labels remain frustratingly undefined. This chapter delves into the nature of situationships, exploring why they arise, how they impact us emotionally, and how to navigate or even exit them. We'll also explore real-life scenarios and equip you with strategies to gain clarity and find emotional fulfilment.

More Than Friends, Less Than Lovers

Lila scrolled through Instagram, a familiar pang of envy twisting in her gut. Photos of loved-up couples flooded her feed, captions proclaiming "forever" and "soulmates." A sigh escaped her lips as she landed on a picture of herself and Alex, arms casually slung around each other at a recent concert. No romantic declaration, just a playful "living our best lives" caption. Their relationship, a tangled mess of stolen glances, late-night texts, and movie nights, was the epitome of a situationship.

It had started innocently enough. Bumping into Alex at their favourite restaurant, their shared love for obscure indie bands sparking a conversation. Laughter flowed easily, and soon, coffee dates turned into Netflix marathons on her couch, punctuated by stolen kisses and lingering touches. But the "what are we?" conversation remained stubbornly lodged in the back of Lila's mind.

Alex was everything she wasn't – a free spirit with a devil-may-care attitude, the complete opposite of Lila's organised, goal-oriented personality. Yet, their differences somehow fit. He challenged her to embrace spontaneity, and she grounded him with her pragmatism.

But the lack of definition gnawed at Lila. Was she just a convenient distraction for Alex, a pitstop in his nomadic existence? Did he feel the same spark, the growing sense of "more" that bloomed within her?

One rainy afternoon, curled up with Alex on her couch, the silence between them grew deafening. Taking a deep breath, Lila blurted out, "We need to talk about this."

Alex, his brow furrowed in surprise, mirrored her sentiment. The conversation, though awkward at first, flowed like a dam breaking. They confessed their fears, their hopes, the growing confusion that mirrored Lila's initial Instagram envy.

What emerged wasn't a clean-cut answer, but a tentative plan. They wouldn't rush into labels, but they wouldn't shy away from defining their wants. Weekends weren't just for casual movie nights; they were for exploring each other's passions, for building a foundation for whatever their future held.

The nebulousness of the situationship remained, but it no longer felt negative. It was a space for exploration, an unspoken agreement to nurture their connection without the pressure of societal expectations.

Months later, on a sunny rooftop overlooking the city, Lila leaned into Alex's shoulder. "So, where do we go from here?" she asked, a playful smile on her lips.

Alex chuckled, his eyes twinkling. "Well, how about we grab some ice cream and figure it out together? One spontaneous adventure at a time."

Lila grinned, the warmth in his eyes more meaningful than any label. Their situationship, messy and undefined, was perfectly imperfect, a testament to the fact that sometimes, the most profound connections defy easy categorisation.

The Enigma of Undefined Relationships

A situationship is essentially a romantic or sexual connection lacking clear labels or a defined trajectory. It exists somewhere in between a committed partnership and a casual hookup, characterised by ambiguity and uncertainty. While some may find this lack of definition liberating, it often leads to confusion, mixed signals, and emotional turbulence.

Examples

The "Seeing What Sticks" Scenario:

Two people enjoy spending time together and engaging in casual intimacy. They text frequently but avoid defining the relationship.

Dates might involve shared activities or simply hanging out, but there's no discussion of exclusivity or commitment.

The "Benefits with Boundaries" Arrangement: This involves a physical connection with the understanding that emotions won't be involved. Both parties are clear about their desire for casual encounters and establish boundaries to avoid misunderstandings. Communication is key to maintaining this dynamic.

The "Keeping Options Open" Mentality: This describes individuals who prioritise dating around to avoid getting tied down. They might see multiple people casually, using texting or apps to connect, but avoid introducing dates to friends or family. This can be a way to explore options before getting serious.

The "Long-Distance Longing" Dynamic: A strong connection forms between two people who are geographically separated. Technology allows them to stay in touch, but the distance makes it difficult to envision a future together. This can lead to feelings of longing and uncertainty.

The Perpetual Maybe: Anya and Vincent, met for the first time at a common friend's party, and hit it off instantly. They spend a lot of time together, enjoying dinners, movie nights, and even intimate weekends. Yet, Anya consistently avoids discussing the future or labelling the relationship. Whenever Vincent attempts to define their status, she deflects, claiming she's not ready for labels. Over time, Vincent feels increasingly anxious and unsure about where he stands, trapped in a perpetual state of "maybe." – Think of it as the romantic version of Schrödinger's cat: the relationship exists in both committed and non-committed states until someone confronts the ambiguity.

The Convenient Lover: Charles and Fiona, colleagues who embarked on a casual sexual relationship, illustrate another situationship scenario. While Fiona was clear about keeping things light, Charles developed deeper feelings. They'd spend nights together and share personal stories, blurring the lines between a fling and something more serious. Despite the intimacy, Fiona insisted they were "just having fun," leaving Charles emotionally conflicted and yearning for more commitment. – Picture the confusion of Ross and Rachel from "Friends," but without the dramatic breaks and makeup. It's a continuous loop of "Are we on a break?"

The Dynamics at Play

Lack of Definition: The core of situationships thrives on ambiguity. The absence of labels allows individuals to enjoy certain aspects of a relationship without the responsibilities or expectations of a committed partnership. This can be appealing for those who fear commitment or are unsure of their feelings.

Mixed Signals: Situationships are notorious for sending mixed signals. One moment the connection feels intense and committed, filled with emotional and physical intimacy, while the next feels casual and nonchalant. This inconsistency creates confusion and emotional strain.

Emotional Investment: Despite the undefined nature, emotional investment often grows. This can lead to a mismatch in expectations and desires, with one or both partners developing deeper feelings. This imbalance can cause frustration, heartache, and a sense of being stuck.

Identifying a Situationship: Red Flags

1. **Ambiguity:** Repeated avoidance of discussions about the relationship's direction or future.

2. **Inconsistency:** Fluctuating behaviour that alternates between intimate and distant.

3. **Lack of Commitment:** Reluctance to make plans beyond the immediate future or introduce each other to friends and family.

4. **Emotional Confusion:** Frequent feelings of uncertainty, anxiety, or dissatisfaction about the relationship.

5. **Convenience Over Connection:** The relationship feels more about convenience than genuine connection or growth.

Charting Your Course: Strategies for Navigation or Exit

Seek Clarity: Open and honest communication is crucial. Express your feelings and ask direct questions about the relationship's direction. Clarity empowers you to make informed decisions about your emotional investment.

Define Boundaries: Establish and communicate your boundaries. Decide what you are comfortable with and what you need for your emotional well-being. This can prevent further emotional confusion and help maintain your self-respect.

Assess Your Needs: Reflect on your own needs and desires. Determine whether the situationship aligns with your long-term goals and emotional health. If it doesn't, it may be time to reconsider the relationship.

Take Action: Based on your reflections and conversations, decide whether to continue, redefine, or end the situationship. Taking proactive steps allows you to regain control over your emotional life and prevent further ambiguity.

Seek Support: Talking to friends, family, or a therapist can provide valuable perspectives and support. They can help you navigate your feelings and offer guidance on making the best decision for your well-being.

The Aftermath: Healing and Moving Forward

Situationships can leave emotional scars, similar to a cliffhanger in a series that never gets resolved. The initial excitement followed by prolonged uncertainty can lead to confusion, self-doubt, and a shattered sense of trust. If you've emerged from a situationship, remember, it's crucial to seek support and engage in self-care to rebuild confidence and emotional resilience. Professional counselling can be particularly beneficial in processing the experience and developing strategies to avoid similar situations in the future.

Conclusion: Embracing Clarity and Self-Awareness

Situationships occupy a complex space in modern romance, blending elements of commitment and casualness into a confusing mix. While some may find this lack of definition liberating, others can experience significant emotional turmoil. By recognising the dynamics and red flags of situationships, individuals can better navigate their relationships and make choices that align with their emotional health and long-term goals. As we continue to explore the intricate dance of love and connection, it is essential to prioritise clarity, communication, and self-awareness. These tools can help us forge relationships that are fulfilling, respectful, and aligned with our true desires.

Remember, the journey towards love is paved with exploration and self-discovery. Don't be afraid to have honest conversations, define your boundaries, and prioritise your emotional well-being. Embrace the lessons learned from situationships, and move forward with a newfound clarity and confidence in your pursuit of genuine connection. As Lewis Carroll reminds us, *"In the end, we only regret the chances we didn't take, relationships we were afraid to have, and the decisions we waited too long to make."* Let this be a catalyst for courage and self-compassion as you navigate the complexities of modern love.

Chapter 5

Bread-crumbing – Giving Someone Just Enough Attention to Keep Them Interested

Welcome back, love adventurers! We've explored the murky territory of situationships, where connections lack clear definition. Let us delve into another perplexing phenomenon: bread-crumbing. Here, someone throws you just enough attention to keep you interested, but never commits to a real relationship. This manipulative behaviour can leave you feeling confused, strung along, and emotionally drained. Let's dissect the art of the bread-crumber, how to identify it, and navigate your way to a fulfilling connection.

From Heartbreak to Masterpiece

Elara, a budding artist with a mane of fiery hair and a head full of dreams, found herself entangled in the frustrating web of bread-crumbing. It all began with Leo, a charming musician with eyes like melted chocolate and a smile that could disarm a dragon. Their first encounter was electric - a chance meeting at a local art fair where Elara's vibrant paintings captivated Leo's attention.

He complimented her work with a genuine enthusiasm that sent a blush creeping up her cheeks. They exchanged numbers, promising to meet again soon. That "soon" turned into a series of sporadic texts - a witty message here, a flirty emoji there, just enough to keep Elara dangling. Dates were elusive, confirmed at the last minute, only to be cancelled with flimsy excuses.

Despite the inconsistency, Elara clung to the hope Leo had ignited. His occasional late-night texts, filled with poetic musings and veiled promises of seeing her "soon," fueled a fire of anticipation. Elara poured her unrequited feelings into her art, the frustration and longing bleeding into vibrant canvases that captured the emotional turmoil within her.

One evening, after a week of radio silence from Leo, Elara received a notification – a photo of him backstage at a concert, with another woman. Jealousy, a bitter aftertaste, flooded her mouth. The truth slammed into her – she wasn't special, just another notch on Leo's charm offensive.

Heartbroken but determined, Elara decided to take back control. She confronted Leo, her voice surprisingly steady. "The mixed signals, the ghosting... it's not fair," she said.

Leo, caught off guard, stammered apologies, blaming his busy schedule. But Elara refused to be fooled. "It's not about time," she stated, her voice firm. "It's about respect. And frankly, I deserve more than bread crumbs."

Ending the conversation, Elara felt a surge of liberation. She poured her heartbreak into a final piece – a portrait of a woman, her back turned, a single tear rolling down her cheek, but her eyes, filled with a newfound resolve.

The painting, titled "Crumbs Won't Feed a Dream," became a local sensation. It resonated with women who, like Elara, had been strung along by love-starved players. Elara, through her art, found her voice, a voice that spoke of strength and self-worth.

As for Leo, Elara never heard from him again. But she didn't need him to validate her worth. She had her art, a growing fanbase, and most importantly, the knowledge that true love wouldn't leave you begging for scraps; it would nourish your soul and fill your life with a love as vibrant and beautiful as the colours on her canvas.

Understanding Bread-crumbing: The Art of the Tiny Nibble

Imagine a hungry bird desperately searching for food. It finds scattered crumbs – enough to tantalise its taste buds but not enough to satisfy its hunger. That's the essence of bread-crumbing. The bread-crumber strategically drops tiny morsels of attention – texts, likes, occasional meet-ups – to keep you engaged and hoping for more. This creates an emotional rollercoaster, leaving you yearning for a deeper connection that never materialised.

Examples: When Fiction Mirrors Reality

The "Almost" Relationship: Remember Monica and Richard from "Friends"? They share undeniable chemistry, passionate encounters, and even a living situation. Yet, Richard hesitates to commit, leaving Monica constantly questioning their status. This "almost" relationship perfectly exemplifies bread-crumbing.

The Social Media Flirt: In the age of digital connections, bread-crumbing can thrive online. Tina, who matches with Owen on a dating app, gets bread-crumbed pretty soon. He sends her witty messages and flirty emojis, keeping her engaged. However, whenever she suggests meeting up, he cites a "busy schedule" or offers vague plans that never materialise.

The Psychology Behind the Crumbs: Why Do They Do It?

Fear of Commitment: Bread-crumbers often fear intimacy and the vulnerability that comes with a committed partnership. By keeping things casual and non-committal, they avoid the emotional risks associated with deeper connections.

Need for Validation: Juggling multiple "almost" relationships provides bread-crumbers with a constant stream of admiration and attention. This inflates their ego and reinforces their sense of self-worth.

Control Issues: bread-crumbing allows individuals to maintain a sense of control over their romantic interactions. By keeping others interested yet emotionally distant, they dictate the pace and dynamics of the connection.

Picking Up the Crumbs of Your Heart: Healing from Bread-Crumbing

The aftermath of bread-crumbing can feel like sifting through the dusty remnants of a pastry, searching for something substantial to hold onto. You're left with a trail of empty promises, fleeting moments of connection, and a heart bruised by the emotional rollercoaster.

Here's how bread-crumbing takes its toll:

1. **Lost in the Maze:** The inconsistent attention and mixed signals create a confusing labyrinth. Are they interested? Not interested? It's impossible to tell, leaving you feeling perpetually off-balance and unsure of where you stand.

2. **A Crumbling Self-Esteem:** The lack of commitment and emotional distance can be a silent weapon against your self-worth. You might start questioning your judgement, wondering if you did something wrong or if you're simply not good enough.

3. **Emotional Rollercoaster:** Bread-crumbing thrives on a cycle of highs and lows. A fleeting text message sparks hope, followed by an agonising silence that leaves you feeling deflated. This emotional whiplash is exhausting and leaves you feeling drained.

Healing takes time, but with self-compassion and a commitment to finding something real, you can move beyond the crumbs and create a love story that truly satisfies your heart's desires.

Breaking Free and Building a Feast: But here's the good news: You don't have to stay chained to the crumb trail. It's time to move on and build a connection that nourishes your soul, a veritable feast for your heart.

Clear the Crumbs: Acknowledge the situation for what it was – an unhealthy dynamic that didn't serve your needs. Let go of the past and focus on the present.

Rebuild Your Confidence: You are worthy of love and respect. Reconnect with yourself, rediscover your strengths, and surround yourself with supportive people who value you for who you are.

Redefine Connection: What does genuine connection look like for you? Prioritise open communication, emotional availability, and mutual respect.

If you suspect you're being bread-crumbed, it's time to take action. Here are some strategies to empower yourself:

1. **Recognise the Signs:** Be aware of the red flags – inconsistent communication, vague commitments, and mixed signals.

2. **Communicate Openly:** Have a frank conversation with the person about the lack of clarity and your desire for a more defined relationship.

3. **Set Boundaries:** Don't settle for ambiguity. Communicate your expectations and needs for a fulfilling connection.

4. **Prioritise Self-Respect:** Don't chase someone who leaves you feeling unimportant and unsure. Walk away from situations that disrespect your time and emotions.

Finding the Real Meal: Cultivating Healthy Connections

Relationships should be nourishing and fulfilling. Here's what to look for in a connection that truly satisfies:

Mutual Respect: Partners value each other's feelings and needs. Communication is open, honest, and consistent.

Reciprocal Effort: Both partners invest time and energy into the relationship. There's a sense of balance and shared commitment.

Emotional Availability: Partners are emotionally present and supportive. They create a safe space for vulnerability and growth.

Remember, love adventurers, you deserve a relationship that offers a full course meal, not just a trail of crumbs. By following these tips, you can empower yourself to find a connection that nourishes your soul.

Invest in Self-Love: Bread-crumbing can chip away at your self-esteem. Rebuild your confidence by focusing on self-care activities that bring you joy and remind you of your worth.

Embrace Clarity: Don't settle for ambiguity. Be upfront about your expectations and needs for a relationship. If someone can't offer consistency and emotional investment, move on. There's someone out there who will appreciate your authenticity and desire for a genuine connection.

Finding Your Tribe - Building a Support System: Don't navigate this journey alone. Surround yourself with supportive friends, family, or a therapist who can offer a listening ear and guidance. Their encouragement and perspective can be invaluable in helping you navigate your emotions and make healthy choices for your well-being.

Remember: You are not alone. Bread-crumbing is a common experience, but it doesn't have to define your love life. By prioritising self-respect, setting boundaries, and seeking healthy connections, you can break free from the cycle of crumbs and build a relationship filled with love, respect, and mutual fulfilment.

Love is a Delicious Adventure: Embrace the Journey

Finding true love is a delicious adventure filled with exploration and discovery. Don't let the fear of getting hurt prevent you from opening your heart to genuine connections. Embrace the lessons learned from bread-crumbing experiences. They empower you to recognise red flags and prioritise your emotional well-being in future relationships.

As Maya Angelou reminds us, *"You may encounter many defeats, but you must not be defeated. In fact, it may be necessary to encounter the defeats so that you can know who you are, what you can rise from, how you can still walk on with your head held high and a style that is your own."*

Chapter 6

Cushioning – The Peril of Playing it Safe

Love adventurers, welcome back! We've navigated the tricky terrains of situationships and the manipulative tactics of bread-crumbing. Let's delve into a realm known as "cushioning." Here, individuals hedge their bets by keeping backup options while seemingly committed to another person. This seemingly "safe" strategy can wreak havoc on trust and emotional well-being in relationships.

No Backups, Just Us

In the bustling city of Metropolis, modern dating became a complex game of swipes and likes. For Emily, a bright and ambitious woman in her late twenties, this game often felt like navigating a minefield of unspoken rules and ambiguous intentions. She had been single for a year after ending a long-term relationship and was now ready to dip her toes back into the dating pool.

One Friday night, Emily matched with Jake on a popular dating app. He seemed charming and shared her love for hiking and coffee. They chatted for a few days before deciding to meet in person. Their first date was a whirlwind of laughter and deep conversation at a cosy cafe downtown. Emily felt an instant connection and thought Jake might be different from the other guys she had met recently.

As weeks went by, Emily and Jake's relationship blossomed. They spent weekends exploring the city, sharing meals, and getting to know each other's friends. Yet, amidst the growing intimacy, Emily couldn't shake a nagging feeling. Jake was attentive and caring, but he seemed to have an unusual number of female friends, with whom he was in constant contact.

One evening, while Emily and Jake were cooking dinner together, his phone buzzed. He glanced at the screen and smiled but didn't mention who it was. Emily's curiosity got the better of her, and she casually asked, "Who's texting?"

"Oh, just a friend," Jake replied nonchalantly. "You know, Pixy from the gym."

Emily nodded, but the unease lingered. Over the next few weeks, similar situations arose. There was always a "Pixy from the gym," a "Megan from work," or a "Lisa from college." Jake assured Emily they were just friends, but she began to notice a pattern.

Determined to understand what was going on, Emily confided in her best friend, Mia. Mia, a seasoned dater, listened patiently before saying, "It sounds like Jake might be cushioning."

"Cushioning?" Emily echoed, puzzled.

"It's when someone keeps potential romantic options on standby while focusing on one primary relationship," Mia explained. "They're basically cushioning themselves against the possibility of the relationship ending, so they're never really alone."

The term struck a chord with Emily. She realised Jake's behaviour fit this description perfectly. While he was sweet and attentive, he always had someone else to text or meet for coffee, just in case things didn't work out with her.

Armed with this new understanding, Emily decided to confront Jake. She needed to know if he was truly invested in their relationship or merely keeping her as a primary option while maintaining backups.

One evening, as they sat in her living room, Emily took a deep breath and said, "Jake, I need to talk to you about something important. I've noticed you're often in touch with other women, and it makes me feel like you're not fully committed to us. Are you cushioning?"

Jake looked taken aback. He paused, clearly grappling with his thoughts. "Emily, I didn't realise it seemed that way. Yes, I do keep in touch with other people, but I never meant to make you feel insecure. I've been hurt before, and I guess I'm scared of being vulnerable again."

Emily appreciated his honesty but knew they needed more than words to move forward. "I understand, Jake. But if we're going to make this work, we both need to be all in. No backups. Just us."

Jake nodded, understanding the gravity of the situation. "You're right, Emily. I care about you, and I want to give us a real shot. I'll cut back on those other connections and focus on what we have."

With that commitment, their relationship took on a new depth. Jake followed through on his promise, and their bond grew stronger. Emily felt more secure and cherished, knowing they were both invested in building something real together.

In the world of modern dating, where options were endless, Emily and Jake chose to prioritise each other, proving that even in a city full of distractions, true connection was still possible.

Understanding Cushioning: The Soft Landing Fallacy

Imagine a tightrope walker, not with a safety net, but with a stack of pillows haphazardly piled below. That's the essence of cushioning. Fearing the potential fall of a broken relationship, someone keeps "backup options" on the sidelines – people they flirt with or maintain connections with in case the primary relationship falters. This behaviour, fueled by insecurity and a fear of commitment, can be incredibly damaging to both parties involved.

When Pillows Become Pitfalls The "Parallel Dating" Approach: Someone might be seriously dating one person but continues to go on dates with others through apps or social circles. This creates a backup plan if things with the primary person fizzle out.

The "Keeping the Flame Alive" Tactic: An individual might maintain contact with an ex or former fling through occasional texts or social media interactions. This could be a way to keep them interested in case the current relationship doesn't work out.

The "Just Friends, Maybe More" Scenario: Someone might become close friends with a potential romantic partner while still actively dating others. This allows them to explore the possibility of a relationship while keeping their options open.

The "Slow Fade" Technique: If someone isn't fully invested in a developing relationship, they might gradually decrease communication and initiate fewer dates. This avoids a direct confrontation but effectively signals a lack of interest while potentially keeping the door open if other options fall through.

The Underlying Motives: Why Do People Cushion?

Fear of Loneliness: The dread of being single can be a powerful motivator. By keeping backup options, individuals attempt to avoid the emotional discomfort of being alone.

Commitment Phobia: The thought of a committed relationship can be overwhelming for some. Cushioning allows them to enjoy aspects of intimacy without the perceived restrictions of a serious partnership.

Insecurity and Low Self-Esteem: Doubting their own worth can lead someone to believe they don't deserve a true and committed relationship. Cushioning provides a false sense of security and validation.

The Price You Pay: The Consequences of Cushioning

Cushioning isn't a victimless act. Here's how it can negatively impact everyone involved:

1. **Erosion of Trust:** If the cushioning behaviour is discovered, it can shatter trust in the relationship. The betrayed partner feels disrespected and deceived, making genuine connection difficult.

2. **Emotional Dishonesty:** Cushioning requires dishonesty – both with yourself and your partner. It prevents genuine intimacy and emotional vulnerability, hindering the growth of a healthy relationship.

3. **Delayed Closure:** Cushioning keeps you from fully investing in your current relationship or properly moving on from past ones. It prolongs emotional ambiguity and hinders personal growth.

If you find yourself cushioning, or suspect your partner might be, it's time to address the issue. Here's how to break free and build trust:

Practice Self-Reflection: Identify the root cause of your cushioning behaviour. Are you afraid of commitment? Do you struggle with low self-esteem? Addressing these underlying issues is crucial.

Embrace Vulnerability: Honest communication is essential. Talk to your partner about your fears and insecurities. True connection thrives on openness and emotional transparency.

Set Clear Boundaries: If you decide to stay in the relationship, establish clear boundaries with your backup options. Distance yourself from flirtatious interactions and focus on building trust with your partner.

Seek Support: Consider individual therapy to address your anxieties and develop healthier coping mechanisms for dealing with relationship challenges.

The Path to Authentic Connection: Embracing Vulnerability

Love adventurers, remember, genuine connection requires vulnerability and a willingness to take risks. While cushioning might seem like a safety net, it ultimately hinders your ability to experience true love and intimacy. By embracing honesty, self-reflection, and open communication, you pave the way for a relationship built on trust, respect, and mutual commitment. Let go of the emotional pillows and step into a love story filled with authenticity and deep connection.

Chapter 7

Orbiting – The Perpetual Social Media Dance

Love adventurers, welcome back! We've delved into the complexities of commitment-phobic behaviours like cushioning. Now, we shift gears and explore the strange phenomenon of orbiting in the digital age. Here, someone lingers on the periphery of your social media, liking your posts and leaving cryptic comments, yet never initiating genuine connection. This confusing dance can leave you wondering: are they interested, or just playing a social media game?

Navigating the Orbit: Finding Clarity in Modern Dating

Annie, a digital marketing specialist in her late twenties, had been navigating the dating world for a while, balancing her career ambitions with the search for meaningful connections.

One evening, Annie met Ron at a mutual friend's rooftop party. He was charming, with a quick wit and an easy smile. They exchanged numbers and began texting daily, sharing everything from their favourite music to their aspirations. Their chemistry was palpable, and after a few weeks, they went on their first date. It was magical, filled with laughter and deep conversation.

However, after that date, things started to shift. Ron's texts became sporadic and his enthusiasm seemed to wane. Annie felt the connection slipping but didn't want to jump to conclusions. She decided to give him some space, hoping he would come around.

Days turned into weeks, and although Ron stopped initiating conversations, he didn't completely disappear. He continued to like Annie's posts on social media, sometimes even commenting on her Instagram stories with witty remarks. Every time she saw his name pop up on her notifications, her heart fluttered with a mix of hope and confusion. It was as if he was hovering around her life, never fully engaging but never completely absent either.

One day, while reading a random magazine Annie came across an article on Orbiting. It instantly raised her eyebrows.

"Orbiting is when someone keeps engaging with you on social media—liking, commenting, watching your stories—without making any real effort to continue the relationship. They stay in your orbit, giving you just enough attention to keep you thinking about them."

The term hit home. Annie realised that's exactly what Ron was doing. He was keeping her on the hook, maintaining a presence in her life without committing to anything substantial.

Determined to take control of the situation, Annie decided to confront Ron. She sent him a straightforward message: "Hey Ron, I've noticed you're still engaging with my posts but haven't made an effort to hang out again. Can we talk about what's going on?"

Ron replied quickly, agreeing to meet for coffee. When they met, Annie was direct. "I need to know where we stand. It feels like you're keeping me in your orbit without really being part of my life."

Ron looked uncomfortable but admitted the truth. "Annie, you're amazing. I guess I wasn't ready for something serious and didn't know how to handle it. I didn't want to let go completely, but I see now that wasn't fair to you."

Annie appreciated his honesty but knew she deserved more. "I understand, but I need someone who's all in, not just hovering around. I think it's best if we go our separate ways."

With that, Annie walked away, feeling a mix of relief and empowerment. She had confronted the confusing behaviour head-on and reclaimed her emotional energy.

In the weeks that followed, Annie focused on herself, enjoying her hobbies, spending time with friends, and diving into new projects at work. She also met new people, both online and offline, with a clearer sense of what she wanted in a relationship.

Understanding Orbiting: A Digital Waltz of Ambiguity

Imagine a satellite perpetually circling a planet, never quite landing. That's the essence of orbiting. Someone you might be romantically interested in, or perhaps even dated briefly, stays connected through social media. They like your photos, leave suggestive comments, and even view your stories. Yet, any attempt at initiating real conversation or asking them out is met with silence or vague responses. This frustrating dance keeps you emotionally tethered, unsure of their true intentions.

When Likes Don't Translate to Dates

The Post-Breakup Orbiter: After a brief fling, Ali continues to like all of Zara's social media posts, occasionally leaving comments like "Looking stunning!" or "Miss our chats!" However, when Zara tries to message him directly, his responses are slow and non-committal. This orbiting behaviour keeps Zara confused, wondering if he wants to rekindle the flame.

The Friend-Zone Orbiter: For years, Daniel has been orbiting Jess, a close friend. He's always the first to like her photos and leaves flirty comments, hinting at something more. Yet, whenever Jess expresses interest in taking things further, Daniel deflects, claiming they're "better as friends." This leaves Jess stuck in the friend zone, perpetually orbiting a potential romance that never takes off.

The Psychological Drivers: Why Do People Orbit?

Several factors contribute to orbiting behaviour:

Attention Seeking: Orbiters crave the validation of likes and comments. They enjoy the feeling of being noticed but lack the courage to pursue a deeper connection.

Fear of Rejection: The digital distance provides a shield against potential rejection. By orbiting, they maintain a sense of connection without risking the vulnerability of asking someone out.

Keeping Options Open: Orbiting allows individuals to maintain a connection with someone they might be interested in, while still exploring other options. It's a way of hedging their bets.

The Emotional Toll: Caught in the Gravity of Ambiguity

Being orbited can be emotionally draining. Here's how it can impact you:

1. **Confusion and Frustration:** The inconsistent behaviour and lack of clarity leave you feeling confused and unsure of the other person's intentions.

2. **Wasted Emotional Energy:** You might invest time and energy wondering what they mean by their likes and comments, leading to emotional fatigue.

3. **Hindered Growth:** Orbiting keeps you stuck in a state of "what if," preventing you from moving on and pursuing genuine connections with others.

Breaking Free from the Orbit - Landing on Solid Ground

If you find yourself being orbited, or suspect someone you're interested in might be doing it, here's how to break free and reclaim your emotional space:

Limit Social Media Interaction: Reduce the temptation to check their profile constantly. Unfollow them if necessary, or mute their updates.

Set Clear Boundaries: If they reach out directly, be upfront about your desire for a real connection, not just social media flirtation.

Focus on Yourself: Invest your energy in activities and relationships that nourish you. Don't let someone's orbiting behaviour define your worth.

The Path to Genuine Connection: Leaving the Likes Behind

Love adventurers, remember, social media validation shouldn't be the foundation of a relationship. True connection thrives on genuine conversation, shared experiences, and emotional vulnerability. Don't get caught up in the orbiting dance. If someone is truly interested, they'll make an effort to connect with you beyond likes and comments.

The world of love and dating may be full of complexities, but by prioritising clarity, communication, and authenticity, you can navigate these challenges and find a love story that's written not in likes and comments, but in shared experiences, mutual respect, and genuine connection. So, dear adventurers, close those social media tabs, put down your phone, and step into the world with an open heart and a clear vision for the love you deserve. Happy exploring, and may your next adventure lead you to a connection that's as exciting and fulfilling as a real-life first date, not just a virtual one!

Chapter 8

Back Benching - The Pain of Being an Option

As we journey further into the intricate dynamics of modern romance, we encounter a particularly disheartening phenomenon: "back benching." This tactic involves keeping someone on standby—valued enough to maintain a connection but not enough to prioritise or commit to. This chapter examines the nature of back benching, its impact on emotional well-being, and strategies for recognising and escaping this manipulative dynamic. Real-life examples will illustrate how back benching operates and the emotional toll it takes on those who find themselves relegated to the sidelines.

A Monsoon Love: Back Benching in the City of Dreams

Mumbai's monsoon rains lashed against the windowpane, mirroring the storm brewing within Akash's heart. He swiped through dating profiles, a familiar ache settling in his chest. Every face was a carefully curated persona; sculpted abs promised adventure, while forced smiles masked a yearning for connection. Then, a profile stopped his scroll. Anjali's picture showcased a bookshelf overflowing with classic literature – a haven for introverts like him. Her bio, simply "Seeking a partner-in-crime for rainy day adventures and literary escapes," felt like a message in a bottle, tossed into the vast ocean of online dating.

Intrigued, Akash sent a message referencing their shared love for a cult classic Hindi novel. To his surprise, Anjali responded with a message filled with insightful commentary and a hint of playful banter. Their conversations flowed like the monsoon rains – refreshing, unpredictable, and brimming with life. They discussed their favourite literary characters, debated the merits of different writing styles, and even confessed their secret desires to write their own stories one day. Akash, usually reserved, found himself opening up to Anjali about his dreams of becoming a screenwriter, a hidden passion nurtured in the quiet corners of his heart.

Their first date was a bibliophile's paradise – a cosy bookstore tucked away in a bustling Mumbai lane. The air thrummed with the comforting scent of old paper as they wandered through the aisles, their conversations echoing amidst towering shelves. Anjali, with her infectious laughter and sharp wit, made him feel seen in a way no one had before. They spoke of their aspirations, their insecurities, and their hopes for the future, creating a tapestry of shared dreams that felt like a story waiting to be written.

But as the monsoon season subsided, a subtle shift began. Anjali's messages, once frequent and filled with literary references, became infrequent and impersonal. Weekend getaways planned with excitement were cancelled with lame excuses. The sting of disappointment was sharp, a stark contrast to the initial warmth. Was this Akash's initiation into the back benches of online dating, reserved for those who didn't quite make the cut?

One chaotic evening, as Akash navigated the crowded Mumbai streets during rush hour, a message from Anjali popped up. It was a picture from a swanky rooftop bar, glittering with fairy lights and overflowing with socialites. Anjali, dressed in a dazzling outfit that felt out of place, had a caption that read, "Living life in the fast lane! Wish you were here."

Akash stared at the picture, the echo of loneliness deafening in his ears. This wasn't the quiet literary date they had discussed; it was a world he wasn't comfortable navigating. With a newfound resolve, he typed a message, not filled with anger or despair, but with a quiet confidence. "Maybe you're looking for a fast-paced story, Anjali. But my heart yearns for a slow burn, like a well-written novel. Here's to happy endings, written in cosy cafes and rainy afternoons."

The silence that followed was deafening, but strangely liberating. Akash had refused to be an afterthought in his own love story. He had chosen to walk away from a connection that promised excitement but lacked depth. Closing the app, Akash felt a surge of strength. Mumbai, the city of dreams, might offer a million possibilities, but he wouldn't settle for anything less than a connection that resonated on a deeper level, a love story that unfolded in the quiet corners of bookstores and rainy days, like the perfect chapter in a well-loved book.

The future remained an unwritten manuscript, but Akash was ready to turn the page. He knew somewhere in the city, amidst the bustling streets and vibrant culture, there existed a reader who would appreciate his quiet strength and love for a good story. A reader who wouldn't relegate him to the back bench, but would join him in writing their own monsoon love story, one chapter at a time.

Understanding Back Benching: Warming the Bench, Not Your Heart

Imagine a crowded sports stadium. The game is on, but you're not in the stands cheering. You're relegated to the back bench – close enough to see the action, but not actively participating. That's the essence of back benching. Someone you're interested in might shower you with initial attention, exciting texts, and even a date or two. However, as time passes, the effort dwindles. They become elusive, communication slows, and plans get cancelled or rescheduled last minute. You're left feeling like an option, not a priority.

Examples

The "Texter, Not a Dater" Scenario: One person consistently initiates texts and calls, expressing interest and setting up dates. However, the other person keeps things casual, frequently cancelling plans or responding with delayed messages, effectively keeping the interested person on hold.

The "Hot and Cold" Dynamic: Someone might shower a potential partner with attention and affection initially. This creates a sense of connection and potential for a serious relationship. However, their interest wanes over time, leading to inconsistent communication and a lack of commitment. They might keep the other person lingering with occasional texts or bread crumbs of affection.

The "Future Fumbler: Discussions about the future are deliberately vague or nonexistent. When the topic of exclusivity or commitment arises, the back bencher might deflect with statements like "We'll see where things go" or "I'm not ready for anything serious right now." This keeps the other person emotionally invested without any concrete progress.

The "Social Media Spotlight" Phenomenon: Someone might readily "like" and comment on their potential partner's social media posts, creating an illusion of interest. However, they rarely initiate real-life interaction or dates, effectively keeping the other person engaged but at a distance.

When Excitement Fades to Frustration

The "Almost There" Texter: After a whirlwind of flirty messages and late-night calls, Will asks Amanda out on a date. The chemistry is undeniable, and they agree to see each other again. However, Will constantly reschedules, citing work commitments. Amanda feels excited one minute, confused and frustrated the next.

The "Maybe Later" Dangler: After a passionate encounter, Rachel tells Mitch she wants to see him again. He expresses interest but keeps pushing dates back, claiming he's "not ready for a relationship." Rachel feels hopeful at first, but as weeks turn into months and his excuses pile up, she realises she's been back benched.

The Motives Behind the Back Bench: Why Do People Do It?

1. **Keeping Their Options Open:** Back benchers are often unsure of what they want in a relationship. They might keep you around as a "backup plan" while exploring other options.

2. **Fear of Commitment:** The thought of a serious relationship can be intimidating for some. Back benching allows them to enjoy aspects of intimacy without the perceived restrictions of commitment.

3. **Insecurity and Emotional Unavailability:** Individuals with low self-esteem might crave attention but lack the emotional capacity to invest in a deep connection.

The Emotional Toll: Stuck in Limbo

Being back benched can be emotionally taxing. Here's how it can impact you:

Confusion and Uncertainty: The inconsistent behaviour of hot and cold signals leaves you unsure of your place in their life.

Diminished Self-Worth: Feeling like an option can chip away at your confidence and self-esteem.

Emotional Drain: The constant hope and disappointment associated with back benching can be emotionally draining and leave you feeling frustrated.

Taking a Stand - Moving from the Back Bench to the Front Row

If you find yourself being back benched, it's time to take action for your emotional well-being:

1. **Communicate Openly:** Have an honest conversation about your desire for clarity. Express your needs and expectations in a relationship.

2. **Set Boundaries:** Don't settle for inconsistent behaviour. If they're not ready for a committed connection, walk away and prioritise someone who values your time and emotions.

3. **Focus on Self-Worth:** Don't let back benching define your worth. Invest in yourself, pursue your passions, and surround yourself with supportive people.

Conclusion: Investing in Your Front-Row Seat

Love adventurers, remember, genuine connection thrives on mutual respect and emotional investment. Don't settle for a back-bench role in someone's life. You deserve to be the leading character in your own love story.

The world of love is filled with adventures, both exhilarating and challenging. By prioritising self-respect, clear communication, and emotional well-being, you'll navigate these experiences with confidence and find a love story worthy of centre stage, not the lonely back bench. So, dear adventurers, hold your head high and step out into the world with an open heart, but a discerning eye. Don't be afraid to walk away from situations that leave you confused and undervalued. Remember, your presence is a gift, and your love deserves to be cherished, not relegated to the sidelines.

Chapter 9

Thirst Trapping – The Allure and Allure-Less of Social Media Bait

Love adventurers, let us now delve into the complex world of social media and a phenomenon known as thirst trapping. Here, individuals strategically post provocative or revealing photos and videos to garner attention and validation, often with the hope of attracting romantic or sexual interest. Let's navigate the murky waters of thirst trapping and explore its impact on self-worth and relationship building.

The Digital Dance: Finding Love Beyond the Likes

Amber stared at her phone, the pool shimmered mockingly behind her. Another perfectly angled bikini shot, pout strategically placed, caption agonising over. "Feeling myself today #beachlife." It was the third thirst trap this week, and a notification popped up – a like from Hugo. A smile played on her lips.

Hugo was new to the dating app. Tall, dark, and with a bio that hinted at a mysterious job that "involved travel." Perfect. Amber swiped right, her carefully curated profile, a mix of travel pics and strategically placed gym selfies, doing its job. They'd messaged for a week, all playful banter and emojis. But no date yet. Maybe this thirst trap would be the push.

Minutes ticked by. No reply. Amber's smile faltered. Just then, her phone buzzed. It was Hugo. "Damn, Amber, you look like fire. When can I take you out and see that for myself?"

Bingo. A giddy excitement bubbled in Amber's chest. "Friday night works for me," she typed, already picturing a night of cocktails, compliments, and maybe a make-out session by the end.

Friday arrived, and Amber prepped like she was going on a runway show. The perfect dress, the right amount of reveal, makeup flawless. Hugo picked her up in a sleek car, a compliment to her image. The night flowed perfectly. Dinner at a trendy spot, Hugo showering her with attention, laughing at her jokes. Yet, a niggling feeling remained.

The conversation never dipped below surface level. Hugo's mysterious job remained just that – a mystery. His compliments were all physical - "That dress looks incredible on you," "Your hair looks amazing." Not a word about her wit, her travel stories, the things she actually cared about.

Later, at a club, Hugo's hand brushed hers a little too low. Amber pulled away, a flicker of annoyance crossing her face. "Easy there, tiger," she said playfully. He chuckled, but the amusement didn't reach his eyes. "Come on, loosen up," he said, voice laced with a hint of entitlement.

Suddenly, the thirst trap felt like a flimsy curtain. It had gotten her here, but it hadn't shown Hugo the real Amber. She excused herself to the bathroom, the reflection staring back at a stranger in a carefully constructed persona.

Back at the table, she met Hugo's gaze. "Actually," she started, voice steady, "I think I'm going to head home."

Hugo's smile faltered. "But the night's just getting started."

"Maybe for you," Amber said, a newfound strength in her voice. "But I'm looking for something more."

The ride home was silent. As Hugo dropped her off, he mumbled something about calling again. Amber just smiled politely, the need for validation replaced by a quiet confidence. Maybe a real connection wasn't found through thirst traps, but through authenticity. Scrolling through her profile later, she deleted the beach pic. Maybe it was time to show the world the real Amber, thirst traps be damned.

Understanding Thirst Trapping: The Like-Fueled Ego Trip

Imagine a fisherman casting a flashy lure into the water, hoping to attract a prized catch. That's the essence of thirst trapping. Social media becomes the fishing ground, and the thirst trap – a scantily clad photo, a suggestive video, or a carefully curated display of physical attributes – is the bait. The goal? To attract an influx of likes, comments, and messages, often from potential romantic or sexual partners.

Real-Life Scenarios: When Likes Don't Equal Love

The Beach Babe Blitz: Every weekend, Chloe bombards her social media with bikini photos, strategically angled selfies, and captions hinting at her availability. While she receives a constant stream of comments and messages from admirers, these interactions are often fleeting and lack genuine connection.

The Mirror-Flexing Mister: Arthur's social media feed is a constant barrage of gym selfies, flexing his muscles and highlighting his physique. He craves the attention and validation from female followers, but struggles to translate this online interest into meaningful relationships.

The Psychological Drivers: Why Do People Thirst Trap?

Several factors contribute to thirst trapping behaviour:

1. **Insecurity and Low Self-Esteem:** Thirst trapping can be a desperate attempt to feel valued and attractive. The validation from likes and comments provides a temporary boost to self-esteem.

2. **Attention Seeking:** For some, the allure lies in the sheer volume of attention, regardless of its quality. Thirst trapping fulfils a need to be seen, noticed, and desired.

3. **Misconstrued Path to Love:** In the age of online dating, some believe that physical attractiveness is the key to attracting a partner. Thirst trapping becomes a misguided strategy for finding love.

The Pitfalls of the Trap - Beyond the Likes

While thirst trapping might bring a temporary ego boost, it can have negative consequences:

Superficial Connections: The focus on physical appearance attracts individuals seeking casual encounters, not genuine connections.

Commodification of Self-Worth: Thirst trapping reduces you to your physical attributes, diminishing your value as a whole person.

Emotional Disconnect: The constant pursuit of online validation can lead to a disconnect from your true self and emotional needs.

Breaking Free from the Bait: Building Self-Worth Beyond the Likes

If you find yourself thirst trapping, or are tempted to, here are some strategies to build self-esteem and seek genuine connection:

1. **Focus on Self-Discovery:** Explore your passions, talents, and interests. Build your confidence based on who you are, not just how you look.

2. **Cultivate Authentic Relationships:** Connect with people who value you for your personality, humour, and intelligence. Invest in quality connections that go beyond the superficial.

3. **Practice Self-Love:** Develop a positive body image and self-acceptance. Celebrate your unique qualities and worth as a person.

Conclusion: Seeking Love, Not Likes

Love adventurers, remember, social media validation is a fleeting high. True love is built on shared interests, mutual respect, and genuine connection. Don't get caught in the shallow waters of thirst trapping.

The world of love and dating is an adventure, filled with exciting connections and potential pitfalls. By prioritising authenticity, self-respect, and the pursuit of genuine connection, you'll navigate these experiences with confidence and find a love story that's filled with substance, not just fleeting likes. Hope you find love that resonates with your true self.

Chapter 10

Gaslighting - The Erosion of Reality

Continuing our exploration into the darker aspects of modern romance, we now turn to gaslighting—a particularly insidious form of psychological manipulation. This chapter delves into the mechanics of gaslighting, examining how it operates, the motivations behind it, and its devastating effects on victims. We'll also provide real-life examples, discuss the red flags to watch for, and offer strategies for recognising and escaping from gaslighting.

Embers of Defiance: Breaking Free from Emotional Abuse

The chipped mug of chamomile tea felt heavy in Léa's hands as she stared at the flickering flames in the fireplace. Beside her, Adam scrolled through his phone, a frown etched on his forehead. Silence, once a comfortable companion, now felt thick and suffocating.

"Is everything alright?" Léa finally ventured, her voice barely a whisper.

Adam glanced up, his expression unreadable. "Fine," he mumbled, dismissing her concern with a flick of his wrist. "Just a long day."

Léa wasn't convinced. Adam's "long days" had become a recent phenomenon, coinciding with a shift in their relationship. His compliments, once plentiful, had vanished. Playful banter had morphed into sharp critiques, often disguised as "constructive criticism." He'd dismiss her achievements as luck, her anxieties as unnecessary worries.

"Remember when I got that promotion?" Léa started, her voice hesitant. "You were so happy for me."

Adam looked up, a flicker of annoyance crossing his features. "I am happy for you, Léa. But let's be honest, it was mostly luck. You were up against interns."

Léa blinked, her chest tightening. It wasn't luck; she'd worked tirelessly for that promotion. But before she could protest, Adam continued.

"Speaking of work, you haven't been your usual self lately. You seem tense, distracted. Maybe that presentation tomorrow is stressing you out."

A knot formed in Léa's stomach. The presentation wasn't due for another week. Adam knew that. Was he trying to make her doubt herself?

The more she questioned Adam's behaviour, the more he'd turn the tables, making her feel insecure and questioning her own memory. He'd deny ever saying hurtful things, insisting she was misremembering or overreacting. He'd call her "too sensitive" or joke about her "dramatics."

Tonight, however, something felt different. A spark of defiance ignited within Léa.

"Adam," she said, her voice surprisingly steady. "We both know the presentation isn't tomorrow. And you know exactly what I'm talking about."

Adam's facade faltered for a moment, a flicker of surprise crossing his face. But then, he recovered quickly.

"Here we go again, Léa," he sighed dramatically. "Twisting my words… Is this really how you want to spend the evening?"

Léa stared at him, her heart pounding. This wasn't a fight; it was a manipulation tactic, a way to deflect blame and make her feel crazy. This wasn't the man she fell in love with.

"No, Adam," she said, her voice firm. "This is how I need to spend the evening. By setting boundaries and realising that your 'constructive criticism' is chipping away at my confidence."

Adam scoffed, but the spark of defiance in Léa's eyes gave him pause. She wasn't the easily manipulated woman he thought she was.

The conversation that followed was difficult, filled with tears and apologies, some genuine, some laced with manipulation. But Léa held her ground. She wouldn't be a victim of his gaslighting any longer.

The relationship, once a source of joy, was now a question mark. But one thing was clear – Léa wouldn't tolerate his emotional abuse anymore. She had found her voice, and she wouldn't be silenced.

The Subtle Sabotage

Gaslighting is a tactic where a manipulator seeks to make their victim question their own reality, memory, or perceptions.

Through a combination of denial, misdirection, contradiction, and misinformation, the manipulator gradually erodes the victim's sense of self and confidence in their own judgement. This psychological warfare creates a dependency on the manipulator, who positions themselves as the sole arbiter of truth.

Examples

The Unfaithful Partner: Jessica was in a relationship with Tom, who was often secretive about his activities. When Jessica expressed concern about his late nights and evasive answers, Tom accused her of being paranoid and controlling. He denied any wrongdoing, even when confronted with evidence, and convinced Jessica that she was overreacting. Over time, Jessica began to doubt her instincts and reality, becoming increasingly reliant on Tom's narrative, despite her growing unease.

Think of Tom as a real-life version of Walter White from "Breaking Bad"—constantly spinning stories and denying his nefarious deeds, making everyone around him question their sanity.

Denial of Events: One partner constantly denies events or conversations that happened, making the other person question their memory. For instance, if they had a discussion about boundaries and later one partner claims it never happened, it can lead the other to doubt their own recollection.

Undermining Self-Confidence: Subtly criticising or belittling the other person's thoughts, feelings, or accomplishments to make them feel inferior. This can be done through statements like, "You're just being too sensitive," or "You're overreacting again."

Shifting Blame: When confronted with their own wrongdoing, the gaslighter shifts the blame onto the other person, making them feel responsible for the problem. For example, if one partner gets caught lying and then accuses the other of being paranoid or distrustful.

Isolation: Gradually isolating the other person from friends and family, convincing them that those people are not good for them or are against their relationship, thereby making the gaslighter the primary source of reality.

Minimising Feelings: Dismissing or trivialising the other person's feelings and experiences. Statements like, "You're just being dramatic," or "It's not that big of a deal," can make the person question the validity of their own emotions.

These tactics can erode the victim's self-esteem and sense of reality, making them increasingly dependent on the gaslighter for validation and truth.

In the Netflix series "You," Joe Goldberg (the protagonist) frequently gaslights his romantic interests, manipulating their perception of reality to maintain control over them.

The Mechanisms of Gaslighting

Denial and Misdirection: Gaslighters often outright deny their actions and statements, even in the face of evidence. This denial creates confusion and self-doubt in the victim, who begins to question their own memory and sanity. Misdirection is also used to shift focus away from the manipulator's behaviour, often by accusing the victim of unrelated issues.

It's like when a magician waves one hand to distract you while the other pulls the trick—classic misdirection that leaves you questioning what you saw.

Contradiction and Confusion: By consistently contradicting the victim's recollections and experiences, gaslighters create a disorienting environment where the victim struggles to discern truth from fiction. This confusion undermines the victim's confidence in their own judgement and makes them increasingly reliant on the manipulator for a sense of reality.

Remember that feeling of disorientation when watching the movie "Inception"? Imagine living that daily because someone keeps twisting your reality.

Trivialising and Minimising: Gaslighters often trivialise the victim's feelings and concerns, making them feel as though their emotions are invalid or exaggerated. This minimises the victim's experiences and reinforces the manipulator's narrative as the more rational and reasonable perspective.

It's like when a celebrity waves off a scandal as "nothing to worry about," leaving their fans and the public bewildered about what actually happened.

Projection and Deflection: Manipulators frequently project their own faults and misdeeds onto the victim, accusing them of the very behaviours they are guilty of. This deflection not only confuses the victim but also shifts blame and scrutiny away from the manipulator.

Imagine Regina George from the series "Mean Girls" accusing Cady of trying to steal her friends, all the while plotting behind everyone's back.

Recognising Gaslighting: The Red Flags

1. **Persistent Doubt:** Constantly second-guessing yourself, your memories, and your perceptions.

2. **Feeling Incompetent:** A pervasive sense of inadequacy and self-doubt, often reinforced by the manipulator's criticism.

3. **Isolation:** A growing distance from friends and family, often due to the manipulator's efforts to cut off your support system.

4. **Apologising Frequently:** An increase in the number of apologies you offer, even when you are not at fault.

5. **Defending the Manipulator:** Frequently defending or rationalising the manipulator's behaviour to others and to yourself.

Strategies for Escape

Reaffirm Your Reality: Keeping a journal of events, conversations, and your feelings can help you maintain a grasp on reality. This record can serve as a reference point when the manipulator attempts to distort the truth.

"The truth is rarely pure and never simple." - Oscar Wilde

Seek External Validation: Talking to trusted friends, family, or a therapist can provide an objective perspective on your experiences. They can help validate your perceptions and offer support.

Imagine having your own personal "Friends" cast—supportive, validating, and always ready to call out any BS.

Establish Boundaries: Set and enforce clear boundaries with the manipulator. This includes limiting interactions and refusing to engage in conversations that undermine your reality.

Educate Yourself: Understanding the tactics of gaslighting can empower you to recognise and resist manipulation. Resources such as books, articles, and support groups can provide valuable insights.

Professional Help: Therapy can be instrumental in rebuilding your self-esteem and confidence. A therapist can help you develop coping strategies and provide a safe space to explore your feelings.

Think of it as hiring your own personal Yoda to help navigate the complexities of your emotional world.

Conclusion

Gaslighting is a deeply destructive form of psychological manipulation that erodes a victim's sense of reality and self-worth. By understanding the tactics and recognising the signs, individuals can protect themselves from this insidious abuse. Escaping from gaslighting requires courage, support, and a commitment to reclaiming your reality. As we continue to navigate the complexities of modern romance, it is crucial to remain vigilant, trust in your perceptions, and seek help when needed. Knowledge and resilience are our greatest allies in the fight against manipulation and emotional turmoil.

So whether you're channelling your inner Eleven from "Stranger Things" to fight back against the mental Demogorgon or seeking clarity like Truman in "The Truman Show," remember: trust yourself, seek support, and reclaim your reality.

Chapter 11

Flashbacking and Fast-Forwarding - Distorting Time and Reality

Hold onto your time-turners, folks! We're diving into the dizzying world of flashbacking and fast-forwarding, where reality takes a spin on the merry-go-round of time and reality.

This chapter delves into the mechanics of flashing back and fast-forwarding in modern dating. We'll explore the motivations behind these tactics, the emotional impact they can have, and how to navigate them with caution. We'll also discuss the importance of setting boundaries and trusting your gut feeling in a world where online personas and curated profiles can distort reality. So, buckle up and get ready to hit pause on the dating app frenzy. It's time to understand the time warps of modern romance and find connections built on genuine communication, not digital manipulation.

Fast Forward, Rewind, Repeat: Breaking the Online Dating Cycle

Amelia swiped through profiles on Tinder dating app - a sense of deja vu washing over her. There he was - Lucas, his profile picture a dazzling smile against the backdrop of a Hawaiian luau. Her heart skipped a little beat. Hadn't they already done this dance?

A year ago, Lucas had been a whirlwind of witty texts and playful banter. They'd bonded over their shared love for sci-fi movies and their disdain for reality TV. The connection had been electric, or so she thought. Then, poof - radio silence. Just like that, Lucas vanished into the digital ether, leaving Amelia with a bruised ego and a lingering sense of confusion.

Now, here he was again, bio unchanged, a new picture the only update. His opening message? A simple "Hey stranger! Remember me?" A flicker of annoyance sparked within Amelia. Here we go again, she thought. The flashback.

Taking a deep breath, she typed, "Vaguely. Weren't you the Hawaiian luau guy?"

Lucas's reply was immediate, filled with apologies about a "crazy family emergency" and claims of never forgetting her. The next few days unfolded like a rerun. Late-night texts, funny memes, and that same familiar spark. Amelia, a sucker for a charming rogue, found herself drawn back in.

But this time, she was more cautious. Lucas's attempts to jump into weekend plans were met with gentle resistance. She insisted on video calls, wanting to see the person behind the perfectly curated profile picture. Lucas, however, seemed hesitant, always finding an excuse – a bad internet connection, a sudden client meeting.

Then, came the fast-forwarder. Sarah, a mutual friend, mentioned a new guy she was seeing – Lucas. Alarm bells clanged in Amelia's head. This wasn't a "crazy family emergency" this time. This was a pattern.

Confronting Lucas was nerve-wracking, but Amelia refused to be played again. She called him out on his disappearing act and his attempt at a rewind. Lucas, caught red-handed, stammered apologies, blaming "commitment issues" and the "pressure of online dating."

Hanging up, Amelia felt a mixture of anger and relief. It wasn't easy, but she had broken the cycle. The flashing back and fast-forwarding tactics wouldn't work on her anymore.

The next morning, she woke up feeling lighter. She deleted Lucas's number and decided to take a break from Tinder. Instead, she messaged Sarah, suggesting a girls' night out – a real, genuine connection, free of digital manipulation.

The Mechanics of Flashbacking and Fast-Forwarding

In modern dating, "flashbacking" and "fast-forwarding" can refer to how people reflect on past experiences or imagine future possibilities within their relationships

"Back to the future" takes on a whole new meaning with flashbacking. It's like being trapped in a Groundhog Day remake directed by your worst nightmare.

While Fast-forwarding in relationships is like hitting the "skip intro" button on Netflix, only to realise you've missed half the plot.

Imagine this: You meet someone online, sparks fly, and the initial conversations are a whirlwind of witty banter and shared interests. You feel a connection you haven't felt in ages. Suddenly, the messages slow down, the calls stop, and you're left wondering what went wrong.

Fast forward a few weeks (or months): A notification pops up - it's them! They apologise for the radio silence, claiming they were "swamped" or "going through a rough patch." They reignite the conversation with the same fiery intensity, making you question if you imagined the whole disappearing act.

This, my friend, is the art of the flashback. They're attempting to rewind the clock and recapture that initial spark, hoping you'll forget the ghosting and jump back on board.

On the other side of the coin, we have the fast-forwarders. These individuals move at breakneck speed, rushing through the initial getting-to-know-you phase and pressuring commitment before you've even had a second date. They might bombard you with messages, suggest weekend getaways, and constantly want to hang out.

Examples

Flashbacking

Reflecting on Past Relationships: Someone might often think about their previous relationships, comparing their ex-partner to their current partner. They might recall past mistakes to avoid repeating them or remember positive experiences to seek similar qualities in a new partner.

Social Media Reminders: Platforms like Facebook and Instagram often show "memories" from past years. Seeing old photos or posts about past relationships can bring back feelings and reflections on how things have changed.

First Date Stories: On a date, individuals might share stories from their past relationships to give context about their dating history, what they've learned, and what they're looking for now.

Fast-forwarding

Discussing Future Plans Early: Early in a relationship, some people might discuss future plans like moving in together, marriage, or having children. This can sometimes be seen as "Fast-forwarding" the relationship to see if long-term goals align.

Dating Apps: When using dating apps, some people might quickly envision what a future with someone might look like based on their profile. They may imagine potential dates, vacations, or life events together before even meeting in person.

Goal Setting: Couples might talk about future aspirations such as career goals, travel plans, or buying a home together, often projecting themselves into these future scenarios to gauge compatibility and shared vision.

Both flashbacking and fast-forwarding are common in dating, as they help individuals understand their past and envision their future, guiding their present relationship decisions.

Spotting the Spin

1. **Constant References to the Past:** When your partner's memory is sharper than Sherlock Holmes', it's time to call for a reality check.

2. **Pressure to Move Quickly:**If your relationship feels more like a race car than a stroll in the park, pump the brakes!

3. **Emotional Whiplash:** Roller Coaster emotions? Check. Dramatic plot twists? Double check. Time to reassess the ride you're on.

4. **Lack of Time for Reflection:** If your relationship feels like a whirlwind tour with no time to stop and smell the roses, it might be time for a pit stop.

5. **Manipulative Nostalgia or Idealisation:** When your partner's idea of romance involves rewriting history, it's time to put on your detective hat.

Strategies for Liberation

Establish Emotional Boundaries: Think of emotional boundaries as the velvet ropes at an exclusive club—only the VIP emotions get in!

Seek External Perspectives: When in doubt, consult the relationship gurus—your friends, family, or even your favourite fictional characters. Because let's face it, Hermione Granger would never put up with this nonsense!

Document Your Experiences: Keep a journal, channel your inner Bridget Jones, and document those manipulative moments like they're juicy gossip for the tabloids.

Assert Your Independence: Remember, you're the leading star of your own rom-com, not a sidekick in someone else's melodrama. Take charge, and don't let anyone fast-forward your story without your consent!

Educate Yourself: Knowledge is power, and in the battle against manipulation, you want to be wielding Excalibur, not a rubber sword from a kid's birthday party.

Conclusion

So, there you have it, folks! By mastering the art of spotting flashbacking and fast-forwarding, you can reclaim control of your narrative, rewrite the script, and emerge as the hero of your own epic saga. Remember, life is too short to fast-forward through the good parts or get stuck in reruns of the bad ones. So, grab your popcorn, buckle up, and get ready for the adventure of a lifetime—because the best stories are the ones we write ourselves! As Terry Pratchett wisely said, *"Time is a drug. Too much of it kills you."*

Chapter 12

Spiralling - The Descent into Emotional Chaos

Welcome to the rollercoaster ride of modern romance, where the highs are exhilarating, and the lows are... Well, let's just say they're a wild ride. Spiralling is like getting stuck in a loop-de-loop of emotional chaos, where the only way out is through.

The Unwinding: Escaping the Emotional Rollercoaster

Arya swiped right, a thrill coursing through her veins like a shot of filter coffee on an empty stomach. Neil's profile was a highlight reel of adventure – white-water rafting in Costa Rica, bungee jumping in New Zealand, all punctuated with a charming grin and a bio that screamed "live life to the fullest!" Their first date was phenomenal – a chaotic exploration of Old Delhi's hidden street food scene, culminating in a breathless ride on a rickety scooter under the starlit sky. Arya felt a spark ignite, a thrilling rush that promised a future filled with adrenaline-pumping experiences.

But the highs, like the sugar rush from a plate of indian mithaais (desserts), were fleeting. Neil's spontaneity often bordered on recklessness. Weekend getaways became impulsive decisions with no regard for budgets, his adventurous spirit masking a fear of commitment. Dates transformed into a rollercoaster of emotions – exhilarating highs followed by crushing lows when Neil, consumed by the next thrill, would disappear for days, leaving Arya feeling adrift.

Flashbacks to simpler times flickered through her mind like silent movie clips. Back in college, love wasn't a performance documented on social media. They were long walks along the Ganges, sharing chai and dreams under the shade of ancient banyan trees. Vivaan, her college sweetheart, had a quiet intensity, his love a steady flame that warmed her heart. Theirs wasn't a rollercoaster romance, but a slow, comforting dance that ended when Vivaan left for his Masters abroad, leaving a void that Arya, seeking excitement, had tried to fill with Neil's whirlwind.

One chaotic evening, after a near miss with a speeding auto-rickshaw during an impromptu bike ride, a stark clarity struck Arya. The constant rush, the emotional loops she was stuck in, were leaving her breathless and exhausted. The woman staring back from her phone screen, pale and exhausted, was a stranger – a far cry from the grounded, independent girl she once was.

Taking a deep breath, Arya ended things with Neil. The silence that followed was deafening, but strangely liberating. It was like stepping off a malfunctioning roller coaster, the world settling back into focus.

The days that followed were a period of self-discovery. Arya reconnected with old friends, rediscovered the joy of quiet evenings spent reading under her favourite peepal tree, and volunteered at a local animal shelter, her laughter echoing alongside the playful barks of rescued pups. Slowly, the vibrant colours of her life began to resurface, replacing the dizzying blur of Neil's world.

Online dating apps remained uninstalled, a reminder of the emotional rollercoaster she'd escaped. Instead, Arya embraced the serendipity of real-life connections. She joined a book club at a local cafe, striking up conversations with fellow bibliophiles over steaming cups of chai. She volunteered at a heritage restoration project, her hands finding solace in the tangible history of her city.

Life, she realised, wasn't a curated profile or a carefully scripted narrative. It was a journey filled with unexpected turns, genuine connections, and the courage to break free from the dizzying loops of emotional chaos. And as the first rays of dawn painted the Taj Mahal in hues of rose and gold, Arya knew her love story was still waiting to be written, each chapter unfolding on its own terms, filled with the quiet joys of self-discovery and the promise of a love that wouldn't leave her breathless, but take her breath away in a whole new way.

The Downward Spiral of Modern Dating

Modern dating can trigger a negative spiral called "spiralling." This involves dwelling on bad experiences, questioning your self-worth, and feeling burnt out from endless swiping. The negativity can lead to risky dating behaviour, social isolation, or giving up altogether. To avoid this spiral, focus on positive experiences, be kind to yourself, take breaks from dating apps, and build a strong social support system. Remember, dating is a journey, and a positive outlook can increase your chances of finding a fulfilling relationship.

Examples

The Emotional Yo-Yo: Picture Samantha's love life as a Tinder date gone wrong. She swiped right on Mark, only to find herself on an emotional rollercoaster with more loops than a psychological thriller series. One minute, Mark was showering her with affection, and the next, he was colder than a polar bear's hug. Samantha couldn't keep up, and before she knew it, she was spiralling into a vortex of self-doubt and confusion. As Oprah Winfrey once said, *"You get a red flag! And you get a red flag! Everybody gets a red flag!"*

The Overthinking Spiral: Endless swiping leads to a focus on negative aspects of profiles. Every detail is scrutinised, fueling anxieties about potential incompatibility. This overthinking can paralyse someone, preventing them from taking the leap to connect and fostering a sense of self-doubt.

The Comparison Trap: Highly curated dating app profiles create an unrealistic standard. Users compare their own (unfiltered) lives to someone's carefully crafted online persona, leading to feelings of inadequacy and missed connections. This can make individuals undervalue their own strengths and overlook genuine compatibility.

The Desperation Cycle: A string of bad dates or rejections can lead to a desperate need for any kind of connection. Standards may drop, leading to matches that aren't a good fit. This cycle of settling can make it harder to find a fulfilling relationship and creates a sense of frustration.

The Social Withdrawal Spiral: After experiencing repeated online dating disappointments, someone might withdraw from social activities entirely. This isolation fuels negativity and makes it harder to meet people organically, creating a self-fulfilling prophecy of loneliness.

The Psychological Mechanisms

Dependency and Isolation: It's like being stranded on a deserted island with only your manipulator for company. By cutting off ties with the outside world, the manipulator creates a sense of dependency that's harder to escape than a Netflix binge-watching session.

Intermittent Reinforcement: Imagine waiting for a message on Tinder, only to get a notification from your manipulator instead. It's like winning the emotional lottery one minute and feeling like you've hit rock bottom the next. No wonder it's harder to leave than a subscription you forgot to cancel!

Gaslighting: Gaslighting is like trying to find your favourite show on TV, only to discover it's been removed without a trace. The manipulator twists reality so much that you start questioning your own sanity. It's enough to make you want to throw your remote at the TV!

Recognising the Spiral - Warning Signs

1. **Emotional Instability:** If your relationship feels like a Netflix original series with more drama than the entire Real Housewives franchise, it's time to reassess.

2. **Isolation:** If you're spending more time with your manipulator than with friends and family, it's a red flag the size of a Hollywood premiere banner.

3. **Loss of Self-Confidence:** When your self-esteem takes more hits than a punching bag in a Rocky movie, it's time to throw in the towel and walk away.

4. **Constant Anxiety:** If your relationship gives you more anxiety than waiting for the next season of your favourite show, it's time to change the channel.

5. **Seeking Validation:** When you're constantly seeking approval from your manipulator like a contestant on a reality TV show, it's time to switch off the drama and focus on reality.

Strategies for Escape

Reconnect with Support Systems: Think of your friends and family as the binge-watching buddies of your life. They're there to provide emotional support and help you navigate the twists and turns of your relationship drama.

Establish Boundaries: Setting boundaries is like hitting pause on the chaos. It's essential to protect yourself emotionally and physically from further manipulation.

Seek Professional Help: Therapy is like having your own personal script doctor. A therapist can help you rewrite the story of your life and reclaim your emotional well-being.

Focus on Self-Care: Self-care is like hitting the reset button on your emotional state. Whether it's yoga, meditation, or a Netflix marathon of your favourite comedy, do whatever brings you joy and peace.

Educate Yourself: Knowledge is power, especially when it comes to recognising manipulation tactics. So, grab your popcorn and dive into the world of self-help books, articles, and podcasts.

Conclusion

Spiralling into emotional chaos is like getting sucked into a reality TV show you never signed up for. But by recognising the warning signs, setting boundaries, and seeking support, you can break free from the drama and reclaim your emotional well-being. Remember, you're the director of your own life, so don't let anyone else steal the spotlight. As Maya Angelou once said, *"When someone shows you who they are, believe them the first time."*

Chapter 13

Ghosting - The Silent Exit

In the realm of modern romance, ghosting has become the disappearing act that leaves us scratching our heads and checking our phones for any sign of life. It's like being left in a room with a magician who forgot to reveal the trick. Let's dive into the mysterious world of ghosting, where closure is as elusive as the Loch Ness Monster.

Silence After Sirens: The Haunting of a Long-Distance Love

The first rays of dawn, deceptively innocent, found Mira spilling a story she never thought she'd share online. A cautionary tale woven with the chilling sting of being ghosted, shattered promises, and a family's dark secret lurking behind a carefully curated Instagram feed. Krish, the man who'd filled her DMs with sweet nothings and promises of forever, was a meticulously crafted illusion, a catfish swimming in the murky waters of the dating world.

Their paths first crossed at a wedding, a fleeting connection that sparked years later when Mira, found herself commenting on Krish's instagram profile. Across oceans, their connection bloomed virtually. Late-night texts replaced stolen glances, emojis stood in for whispered sweet nothings – a sweet romance conducted entirely through the glow of a phone screen. Love, or at least the intoxicating illusion of it, blossomed. Krish, the master of online charm, confessed his undying devotion through perfectly crafted paragraphs. Mira, wary of the distance and the lack of video calls, offered a hesitant response.

It was Krish who then dangled the solution – "Come visit me so we can spend some time together." Blinded by the prospect of a future together, a future meticulously documented on a shared Pinterest board, Mira booked a flight across continents. She arrived in New York, met Krish who was extremely charming and everything seemed too good to be true. Mira instantly hit it off with Krish. The initial days were a carefully staged performance. Krish, the consummate host, whisked her away to a beautiful house he claimed as his own. He took her to all the places they spoke about on the phone. They devoured exotic meals at some of the best New York cafes and restaurants. She met his carefully chosen circle of friends (all suspiciously active on his social media), explored pre-selected gems, and documented their stolen moments of intimacy with strategically angled selfies. Entranced, Mira extended her stay, a decision tinged with a growing disquiet about his uncertain immigration status and his curious state of being unemployed. Despite the whispers of doubt, she clung to the illusion, yearning for the happily-ever-after their online connection promised.

As the holidays got over, Mira returned home. Their "long-distance romance" continued for a few months, fueled by a constant stream of texts and endless calls. Then, the radio silence. Calls went unanswered, texts delivered the dreaded "read" notification but no response. The charming facade crumbled, revealing a hollowness as vast as the digital space that had once connected them.

Mira, ghosted not just by Krish but by his entire online presence, refused to be a victim. Devastated, yes, but her spirit remained unbroken. A chance encounter with an influential friend who heard Mira's sad story - proved pivotal. He saw the cracks in Mira's story, the gnawing suspicion mirroring the one that had taken root within him. He delved deeper, unearthing a truth that left Mira reeling. Krish, far from the devoted lover he portrayed, was already married, had scammed many other women, his immigration status was illegal without valid work authorisation, he laundered money along with his family members, and committed many other fraudulent schemes. His charming facade was a mask for a serial online deceiver and a con artist. Mira, just one of his many victims.

The betrayal cut deep, a wound that festered with the knowledge of Krish's family's complicity. They offered no solace, no apology, only the chilling silence of their online blackout. Armed with the weight of evidence and the stories of other women he had wronged, Mira sought justice. She filed complaints, exposing the truth on social media, a public forum where his web of lies had thrived. But unlike a fairytale ending, there was no dramatic confrontation, no tearful apology, no grand gesture of remorse. Krish and his family simply vanished from the digital world, leaving Mira to sift through the wreckage of her shattered online dreams.

The ethereal glow of dawn, however, held a new promise for Mira. It marked a new beginning, not an ending. The ghost of Krish might linger in the recesses of her memory, but it wouldn't define her. Her story, a testament to unwavering resilience, would become a beacon for others caught in the treacherous currents of online deception. Mira, though scarred, remained unbroken. She was ready to turn the page, to write a new chapter in the real world, a love story built not on carefully curated feeds, but on the bedrock of honesty and genuine connection.

Ghosting: The Haunting of Modern Dating

Ghosting, in the context of modern dating, refers to the practice of abruptly ending all communication with someone you've been romantically or casually involved with, without any explanation. It can happen over text, phone calls, dating apps, or even in person. Someone you were talking to regularly simply vanishes. It's like disappearing into thin air, leaving the other person confused, hurt, and often questioning their own worth.

Examples

The Fizzle Fade: You've had a few fun dates with someone, the conversation flowed easily, and there seemed to be potential. Then, after the last date, texts take longer and longer to get replies, calls go straight to voicemail, and you're eventually left hanging with no explanation.

The Slow Disappear: You've been talking to someone online for a while, exchanging messages daily and getting to know each other. Suddenly, the messages become less frequent, taking days to get a response. Eventually, they stop altogether, and you're left wondering what happened.

The Post-Hookup Poof: You have a seemingly successful casual encounter with someone. You agree to meet up again, but then radio silence. No response to texts or attempts to make plans, leaving you feeling used and confused.

The Committed Ghost: You've been in a seemingly stable relationship for months, maybe even years. Then, out of the blue, your partner stops responding to your messages and calls. They disappear without a word, leaving you heartbroken and bewildered.

The Post-Argument Fade-Out: You have a disagreement with your partner, and things get heated. Instead of communicating, they simply stop responding to your attempts to talk it out. This silent treatment can be a form of ghosting within an established relationship.

The Psychology of Ghosting

Avoidance of Conflict: It's like avoiding the final boss battle in a video game, except in this case, the boss battle is a difficult conversation about feelings. By ghosting, the ghoster chooses to press pause on the conflict and disappear into the digital ether.

Fear of Emotional Repercussions: Ghosting is like hitting the eject button on an emotional rollercoaster before it goes off the rails. The ghoster fears the other person's reaction and would rather vanish than face the fallout of a breakup.

Lack of Accountability: In the age of online dating and digital connections, ghosting has become the ultimate escape hatch. It's like swiping left on a relationship without any consequences or accountability. Out of sight, out of mind, right?

The Impact of Ghosting

Emotional Confusion: Ghosting leaves the ghosted individual feeling like they're stuck in a Choose Your Own Adventure book with no page numbers. Without any explanation, they're left to navigate the maze of their emotions alone, wondering what went wrong.

Loss of Closure: Closure becomes as elusive as the Loch Ness Monster. Without it, the ghosted individual is left with more questions than answers, replaying past conversations like a broken record in search of closure that may never come.

Damage to Self-Esteem: Being ghosted is like getting a rejection letter from Hogwarts, it stings, and it makes you question your worth. The abrupt rejection can leave scars on self-esteem that take time to heal.

The Red Flags - Recognising and Responding to Ghosting

1. **Inconsistent Communication:** When the other person's replies become as sporadic as a squirrel on caffeine.

2. **Avoidance of Plans:** When making future plans feels like pulling teeth that are painful and fruitless.

3. **Lack of Engagement:** When their messages go from Shakespearean sonnets to one-word responses.

Coping Strategies

Accept the Reality: It's time to face the music and accept that you've been ghosted. Sometimes closure is a luxury we can't afford, so it's time to move on.

Reflect on the Relationship: Take a deep dive into the relationship and examine any red flags you might have missed. It's like rewatching a movie to catch all the hidden Easter eggs.

Seek Support: Turn to your squad for some emotional backup. They'll provide the support and validation you need to get through this rough patch.

Focus on Self-Care: Treat yourself like the main character in your own love story. Engage in activities that bring you joy and remind you of your worth.

Move Forward: Remember, you're the author of your own story. It's time to turn the page and start a new chapter - one that's ghost-free and filled with possibilities.

Conclusion

Ghosting may leave us feeling abandoned and confused, but understanding its psychology and impact can help us navigate the murky waters of modern romance. By recognising the signs, employing coping strategies, and focusing on self-care, we can emerge from the ghosting experience stronger and more resilient. As we continue on our quest for love and connection, let's remember to prioritise open communication, mutual respect, and emotional honesty to build healthier and more fulfilling relationships. After all, closure may be elusive, but self-love is always within reach.

"The truth is, unless you let go, unless you forgive yourself, unless you forgive the situation, unless you realise that the situation is over, you cannot move forward." - Steve Maraboli

Chapter 14

Uncoupling – Unveiling the Relationship's Act

Uncoupling isn't just about tossing your relationship into the Netflix queue and hitting play on "It's Complicated." It's a carefully choreographed dance of emotions, decisions, and shared responsibilities, akin to planning the ultimate Hollywood blockbuster.

Rewriting Love

Tara sat in her favourite corner of the cafe, nursing a latte as she stared out the window at the bustling street below. The world moved on, indifferent to the quiet turmoil brewing inside her. She glanced at her phone, half-expecting a message, but the screen remained stubbornly blank. It had been three days since she and Dev decided to uncouple.

Modern dating was supposed to make things easier. Apps, websites, and social media platforms promised endless opportunities and perfect matches. But Tara had found that more options often led to more confusion. She and Dev met on a popular dating app, their profiles perfectly curated to attract each other. Their initial dates were a whirlwind of excitement, shared interests, and the thrill of new love. Yet, as the months passed, the sheen began to fade.

They had tried to make it work. Conversations about the future became common, but so did arguments about career choices, personal goals, and the increasingly blurred lines between their virtual and real lives. They followed all the advice – communicating openly, setting boundaries, and giving each other space. But something was missing, a crucial connection that no app algorithm could predict or create.

When Dev first brought up the idea of uncoupling, Tara was taken aback. It wasn't a breakup, he explained, but a conscious decision to step back and evaluate their relationship outside the pressures of a traditional romantic commitment. It was a modern approach, popularised by celebrities and relationship experts, meant to offer clarity and prevent the resentment that often brewed in struggling partnerships.

They decided to give it a try. They redefined their boundaries, agreeing to see other people, but also to remain a part of each other's lives. It was confusing at first – the shift from exclusive partners to something more ambiguous. Tara downloaded the dating apps again, swiping through profiles with a mix of curiosity and hesitation. She met new people, went on a few dates, but her heart wasn't in it. She missed Dev.

As the weeks passed, the distance provided some clarity. Tara began to focus more on her own life, her hobbies, and her friendships. She realised how much she had leaned on Dev for happiness, neglecting her own needs and desires. It was liberating, but also lonely.

Dev, on the other hand, seemed to thrive. He took up new hobbies, travelled, and even posted pictures with new faces on social media. It stung to see him move on so easily, but Tara reminded herself that this was part of the process. They had agreed to this uncoupling to grow, to find themselves, and to understand what they truly wanted.

One evening, as Tara sat in her apartment scrolling through old photos of them, her phone buzzed. It was a message from Dev: "Hey, can we talk?"

They met at the same cafe where Tara now sat, her heart pounding with anticipation. When Dev walked in, he looked different – more confident, more at peace. They ordered their usual drinks and settled into a booth.

"I've been thinking a lot," Dev began, his eyes searching hers. "About us, about what we had and what we were missing."

Tara nodded, her throat tight. "Me too."

Dev took a deep breath. "I think we lost ourselves in each other. We were trying so hard to be perfect for one another that we forgot to be true to ourselves."

Tears welled up in Tara's eyes, but she smiled. "I've realised that too. I've been focusing on myself, and it's been…eye-opening."

They talked for hours, laying everything out on the table. The uncoupling had given them the space to grow individually, to address their own needs and desires. They had both changed, and it was clear that their relationship would never be the same.

But that wasn't necessarily a bad thing.

As they left the cafe, the sun setting behind them, they made a pact to rebuild their relationship on new terms. They would take it slow, respecting each other's individuality while cherishing the connection that had brought them together in the first place.

In a world of endless choices and fleeting connections, Tara and Dev found a way to navigate the complexities of modern dating. Uncoupling had given them the clarity to understand that love wasn't about perfection, but about growth, understanding, and the courage to redefine what it meant to be together.

The Breakup Revolution: Why Uncoupling is the New Black

Uncoupling describes the process of separating from a romantic partner in a conscious and amicable way. It's a more nuanced approach than a traditional breakup. Uncoupling promotes a mature and mindful approach to ending a relationship. By prioritising respect, communication, and healing, couples can navigate this difficult transition with greater emotional clarity and pave the way for a healthier future, both individually and potentially as co-parents.

Examples

The Shifting Priorities Split: After five years together, a couple realises their career ambitions and life goals have diverged significantly. They acknowledge their love and the happy memories, but agree that their long-term visions are incompatible. Through open communication, they create a plan for dividing assets and establish clear boundaries for future interactions. Though no longer a couple, they end the relationship with respect and well-wishes for each other's future success.

The Co-Parenting Collaboration: A married couple with young children acknowledges the fading spark in their romantic relationship. However, they prioritise the well-being of their children and decide to uncouple through co-parenting collaboration. They attend therapy sessions together to navigate the emotional complexities and create a clear parenting plan. While their romantic connection has shifted, they prioritise respectful communication and teamwork for the sake of their children's stability.

The Fading Flame: Two individuals in a passionate but short-lived relationship realise their initial intensity is unsustainable for the long term. Honest conversations reveal a lack of deeper connection. They agree to gradually spend less time together, leading to a natural decrease in communication. Eventually, the relationship fades organically without resentment, allowing them to move on with a sense of closure.

The Supportive Long-Distance Disentanglement: A same-sex couple in a long-term relationship receives career opportunities in different cities. Despite strong affection, they acknowledge the challenges of maintaining a long-distance relationship. They choose to uncouple with support and understanding. They remain invested in each other's successes, celebrating milestones and offering emotional support despite the physical distance. Uncoupling allows them to prioritise their personal growth while maintaining a foundation of respect and friendship.

"Conscious uncoupling is the ability to understand that every irritation and argument was a signal to look inside ourselves and identify a healing opportunity." - Gwyneth Paltrow

Stages of Uncoupling: From Action to Credits

Awareness: Lights, Camera, Acknowledge: The opening scene sets the stage for the breakup drama. It's time to face the music and admit that the relationship isn't exactly winning any Oscars. Cue the emotional montage of self-reflection and contemplation.

Communication: Dialogue, Drama, Discussion: In this pivotal scene, the protagonists sit down for the heart-to-heart conversation to end all heart-to-heart conversations. It's a battle of words, emotions, and raw vulnerability as they lay their cards on the table. Cue the tissues and dramatic music.

Decision-Making: Negotiation, Compromise, Closure: As the plot thickens, it's time to make the tough decisions. Who gets the Netflix password? Who keeps the beloved pet goldfish? It's a rollercoaster of negotiations and compromises, but in the end, both parties emerge with a sense of closure. Cue the resolution and fade to black.

Transition: Moving On, Moving Out, Moving Forward: As the dust settles, the protagonists embark on the next chapter of their lives. It's a time of adjustment, adaptation, and newfound independence. Cue the montage of packing boxes, tearful goodbyes, and hopeful new beginnings.

Healing: Redemption, Reflection, Rebirth: In the final act, the protagonists emerge from the wreckage of their failed relationship stronger, wiser, and ready for whatever the future holds. It's a journey of self-discovery, growth, and healing as they embrace their newfound independence and embark on the next chapter of their lives. Cue the triumphant music and roll credits.

Emotional Challenges of Uncoupling

Grief and Loss: Tears, Tissues, Transformation: As the reality of the breakup sinks in, the protagonists grapple with feelings of loss and sorrow. It's a tumultuous journey of tears, tissues, and emotional upheaval as they mourn the end of their relationship and the dreams they once shared.

Fear and Uncertainty: Doubt, Dread, Discovery: Amidst the wreckage of their failed relationship, the protagonists confront their deepest fears and insecurities. It's a battle of doubt, dread, and existential crisis as they navigate the uncertain terrain of life after uncoupling.

Guilt and Regret: Remorse, Reflection, Redemption: Haunted by memories of their failed relationship, the protagonists grapple with feelings of guilt and regret. It's a journey of remorse, reflection, and redemption as they confront their past mistakes and seek forgiveness.

Strategies for Navigating Uncoupling: The Director's Cut

Seek Support: Cast and Crew, Counsel and Comfort: In times of emotional turmoil, the protagonists turn to their trusted support network for guidance and solace. It's a journey of healing, growth, and self-discovery as they lean on their friends, family, and therapist for support.

Maintain Respect: Dignity, Decorum, Divorce: Amidst the chaos of their failed relationship, the protagonists strive to maintain a sense of dignity and decorum. It's a journey of mutual respect, empathy, and understanding as they navigate the emotional minefield of uncoupling.

"Respect is one of the greatest expressions of love." - Don Miguel Ruiz

Establish Boundaries: Walls, Windows, Wisdom: In the aftermath of their breakup, the protagonists set clear boundaries to protect their emotional well-being. It's a journey of self-preservation, empowerment, and liberation as they reclaim their independence and autonomy.

Focus on Self-Care - TLC, Treats, Transformation: In the midst of their emotional upheaval, the protagonists prioritise self-care and self-love. It's a journey of healing, growth, and self-discovery as they indulge in acts of self-compassion and self-kindness.

Reflect and Learn: Lessons, Legacy, Liberation: As the dust settles on their failed relationship, the protagonists reflect on the lessons learned and the legacy left behind. It's a journey of self-discovery, growth, and transformation as they glean wisdom from their past mistakes and embrace the promise of a brighter future.

Conclusion: The Final Curtain Call

Uncoupling is a journey of self-discovery, growth, and transformation, but when approached with intention and grace, it can lead to a brighter, more fulfilling future. By recognising the stages of uncoupling, addressing emotional challenges, and employing strategies for navigating the journey with dignity and respect, the protagonists emerge stronger, wiser, and ready for whatever the future holds.

As we bid farewell to the protagonists of our breakup drama, let us remember that every ending is also a new beginning, and every setback is an opportunity for growth and transformation. May we all find the courage to navigate the twists and turns of life with grace, resilience, and an unwavering commitment to self-love and self-discovery. After all, the show must go on!

"Some things become more valuable when broken. Like hearts, relationships and the broken hearts of people in these broken relationships." - Priya Malik

Chapter 15

Zombieing – When Someone Resurfaces from the Past After Ghosting

Welcome back, love adventurers, to another intriguing chapter of "Love Games: Decoding Modern Romance." Let us dive into the chilling world of "zombieing," where someone who previously ghosted you resurfaces unexpectedly. Just like a zombie rising from the dead, this person reappears in your life, often causing confusion and emotional turmoil. Let's explore this phenomenon with examples from popular culture, celebrity scenarios, and insightful quotes.

The Art of Closure

A flicker of annoyance crossed Mia's face as the notification blinked on her phone screen. It was a friend request – from Paul. Her pulse quickened, a jolt of something akin to fury and disbelief. Paul, the charismatic writer who'd filled her days with whispered sonnets and stolen moments under fairy lights strung across his balcony, the one who'd vanished into the digital ether six months ago.

Memories flooded back – their late-night conversations fueled by tea simmering on the stove, the way his touch sent shivers down her spine, the deafening silence that followed his abrupt disappearance. No calls, no texts, just a void where their budding connection used to be. Mia, heartbroken and confused, had poured her hurt into vibrant paintings and tear-stained canvases.

Now, here he was, a spectral presence requesting re-entry into her life. Clicking on his profile, Mia saw pictures – Paul grinning with new colleagues at a book launch, strolling through a bustling literature festival, holding a gleaming award for a local writing competition. A bitter laugh escaped her lips. He'd been basking in his literary acclaim while she'd been piecing together the fragments of her shattered heart.

The anger simmered, but a sliver of curiosity flickered too. Did he expect her to forget everything, to welcome him back with open arms? Mia pictured a witty, scathing message, a digital takedown that would leave Paul reeling. But then, a different thought emerged.

Revenge was a dish best served cold, and what could be colder than a calculated, indifferent response? With a smirk, Mia accepted the friend request.

The next few days were a masterclass in passive aggression. Mia posted photos with her friends, cryptic captions hinting at a budding new creative project. She shared articles about the importance of self-respect and the dangers of online connections. Paul, predictably, started "liking" her posts. Mia resisted the urge to comment, instead revelling in the silence.

One evening, a message popped up – from Paul. "Hey Mia, long time no see! How are you?"

Mia crafted her response with care. "Hey Paul, I'm doing well, thanks! Busy chasing creative dreams, you know?" Short, polite, devoid of any lingering feelings.

Days turned into weeks, and Paul's attempts at initiating a conversation became more frequent. Mia held firm, her replies polite but distant. Finally, frustrated, Paul sent a message: "Look, I know I messed up. Can we talk?"

This was it. The moment Mia had been waiting for. She typed a single line: "Maybe. But not on social media."

Paul's number, thankfully, hadn't been deleted. A deep breath, and Mia hit a call. The phone rang, then Paul's voice, a touch hesitant.

They talked. Not with anger, but with a strange sense of clarity. Paul apologised profusely, his excuses lame, but his remorse genuine. Mia listened, then spoke her truth, the hurt, the confusion, the anger she'd carried for months.

By the end of the call, a strange understanding hung in the air. Paul wouldn't be returning from the digital graveyard. Their connection, like an unfinished painting, would remain in the past. There was no grand gesture, no promise of a future together. Just a quiet goodbye, a respectful closure.

Hanging up, Mia felt a weight lift from her chest. The ghost of Paul had finally been laid to rest. And while the experience left a scar, it also brought a newfound strength. Mia knew, with a fierce certainty, that her artistic spirit wasn't dependent on someone else's validation. She was done being ghosted, and she wouldn't settle for anything less than a connection that wouldn't disappear with a click.

Understanding Zombieing

Zombieing occurs when a person who has ghosted you suddenly reappears in your life, attempting to reconnect as if nothing happened. This behaviour can be perplexing and emotionally destabilising, as it forces you to confront unresolved feelings and questions about the relationship.

Examples

The Social Media Like Resurrection: The silence stretched on for months. Radio silence. Then, a notification pops up – a "like" on a recent travel photo. It's from a familiar, yet unwelcome name - your ghosted ex. Confusion washes over you. Was it an accidental click, or a calculated attempt to re-enter your digital world? The like hangs there, a digital zombie, a reminder of the unresolved ending.

The Accidental Text Blunder: Blocking your ex felt empowering, a clean break from the negativity. Weeks later, a text arrives with a familiar, apologetic tone. "Hey, so sorry about the fight the other day..." The message stops abruptly. Wait, this isn't your current number! A wrong digit reveals your ex's attempt to reach out, leaving you to wonder if it was a genuine mistake or a clumsy attempt to re-initiate contact.

The Convenient Swipe Right: Months after ghosting you, your ex's profile reappears on your dating app. The bio remains unchanged, but a cheesy pick-up line replaces the blank message. Is this a genuine attempt to reconnect, or a tactic to boost their own dating prospects? The reappearance feels manipulative, a reminder of why you swiped left the first time.

The Birthday Text Enigma: A year of radio silence. Then, on your birthday, a notification pierces the quiet – a text from your ex with a generic "Happy Birthday!" The timing feels suspicious, a birthday wish seemingly pulled from the internet, not from a place of genuine care. Is it a test to see if you're still interested, or simply a convenient way to re-enter your life?

The Post-Breakup Party Ploy: You ended things amicably, but the incompatibility was undeniable. A month later, an invite arrives – a party hosted by your ex's friend group. The invite feels like a veiled invitation, a test to see if you're open to reconnecting in a social setting. This unexpected social media interaction leaves you wondering if attending would be awkward or a chance for closure.

The Return in "Sex and the City": In the iconic series "Sex and the City," Mr. Big frequently ghosts Carrie Bradshaw, only to reappear in her life multiple times. Each re-entry leaves Carrie in emotional turmoil, as she grapples with her unresolved feelings for him and the pain of his previous disappearances.

"Maybe our mistakes are what make our fate. Without them, what would shape our lives? Perhaps if we never veered off course, we wouldn't fall in love, or be who we are." – Carrie Bradshaw, "Sex and the City"

Celebrity Comebacks: Justin Bieber and Selena Gomez had a famously tumultuous relationship, marked by periods of silence and sudden reappearances. Their on-again, off-again dynamic illustrates the emotional rollercoaster of zombieing, where past partners resurface, reigniting old feelings and complications.

"Sometimes, you just have to let go of what you thought your life would be like and embrace the life that is waiting for you." – Justin Bieber

The Psychology of Zombieing

Zombieing often reflects a mix of personal indecision, fear of commitment, and the need for emotional validation. Individuals who engage in this behaviour may not fully understand the impact of their actions on the people they re-enter.

Fear of Missing Out (FOMO): The fear of missing out on a potentially meaningful connection can drive people to reappear in the lives of those they previously ghosted. They might feel a sense of regret or curiosity about what could have been.

Emotional Validation: Zombieing can also stem from a desire for emotional validation. By re-establishing contact, the individual seeks reassurance of their worth and significance in the other person's life.

Indecision and Regret: Indecisiveness and regret play significant roles in zombieing. The person may have ghosted due to uncertainty or personal issues but later regretted their decision, prompting them to re-establish contact.

The Emotional Impact of Zombieing

Zombieing can have a profound emotional impact on the person being re-engaged. It often stirs up unresolved feelings, trust issues, and confusion, making it difficult to navigate the re-emergence.

1. **Trust Issues:** When someone who ghosted reappears, it can severely damage trust. The person being zombied may struggle to believe that the individual won't disappear again, leading to hesitation and doubt.

2. **Emotional Confusion:** Zombieing can lead to significant emotional confusion. The reappearance of a past partner can reignite old feelings, making it difficult to discern whether these emotions are genuine or a response to the sudden contact.

The unexpected reappearance of someone who ghosted can force individuals to confront unresolved feelings and questions about the relationship. This process can be emotionally taxing and destabilising.

Navigating Zombieing

Dealing with zombieing requires a balance of self-awareness, clear communication, and emotional resilience. Here are some strategies to navigate this challenging dynamic.

Assess Your Feelings: Take time to assess your feelings about the person's reappearance. Reflect on whether you genuinely want to reconnect or if your emotions are driven by the suddenness of their return.

Set Boundaries: Establish clear boundaries to protect your emotional well-being. Communicate your expectations and limits with the person who has reappeared, ensuring they understand the impact of their previous actions.

Communicate Honestly: Have an honest conversation with the person about why they ghosted and why they are reappearing now. Understanding their motivations can help you decide whether to give them another chance.

Prioritise Self-Care: Focus on self-care and emotional healing. Engage in activities that bring you joy and peace, and seek support from friends, family, or a therapist if needed.

"The most powerful relationship you will ever have is the relationship with yourself."– Steve Maraboli

Evaluate the Relationship: Consider whether the relationship is worth re-establishing. Reflect on past dynamics and whether they have the potential for a healthy future. Trust your intuition and prioritise your emotional health.

Conclusion

Zombieing is a perplexing behaviour that can leave emotional scars and disrupt the healing process from past relationships. By understanding the psychology behind zombieing, recognising its emotional impact, and employing strategies to navigate it, you can protect your emotional well-being and make informed decisions about re-engaging with past partners.

As we continue to explore the complex dynamics of modern romance, remember that every relationship deserves clarity, respect, and genuine effort. Stay true to yourself, prioritise your well-being, and seek connections that bring positivity and growth into your life.

Chapter 16

Paperclipping – Reconnecting with an Ex When They Have a New Partner

Let us look into another insightful chapter. Here, we examine the perplexing behaviour known as "paperclipping," where someone reconnects with an ex-partner just when that ex has moved on to a new relationship. This phenomenon can stir up complex emotions and challenge the stability of current relationships. Let's delve into this tactic with relatable real-life examples and thought-provoking quotes.

A Knock in the Past

The rhythmic tap-tap-tap of Jacob's fingers against the worn leather steering wheel echoed the frantic beat of his heart. He shouldn't be here. Not outside her apartment building, not two years after their tearful goodbye. But the news, a cruel twist of fate, had propelled him across town, a desperate need to see her face clouding his judgement.

Rachel - The woman who'd painted his world with vibrant hues of laughter and adventure, only to have it all washed away by the harsh reality of his career ambitions. He'd chosen the prestigious law firm in New York, chasing a future they'd both dreamt of, a future that ultimately fractured their love story.

Then, silence. Radio silence. No angry calls, no pleading texts, just a void that echoed louder than any scream. He'd tried to move on, the ache in his chest a dull throb he'd grown accustomed to. Until yesterday, when a social media post, a picture of Rachel beaming next to a man with kind eyes and a warm smile, had shattered the carefully constructed walls around his heart.

Jacob parked the car, his breath fogging in the crisp autumn air. He wrestled with the urge to flee, to return to the predictable rhythm of his life in New York. But his feet, guided by an invisible force, carried him towards the familiar brownstone building.

He hesitated at the door, the familiar scent of jasmine from a nearby flower shop sending a shiver down his spine. Finally, he pressed the buzzer for Rachel's apartment.

The wait felt like an eternity. Then, her voice, a melody he hadn't heard in far too long, crackled through the intercom. "Hello?"

"Rachel," he rasped, his voice thick with emotion. "It's Jacob."

A beat of surprised silence, then the click of the door unlocking.

He climbed the stairs, each step a physical manifestation of the emotional turmoil within. When he reached her door, he took a deep breath and knocked. The door swung open, revealing Rachel.

She looked different, a maturity etched on her face, but her eyes, those beautiful eyes that had held his universe, still held the same warmth. A man, the one from the picture, stood beside her, a questioning look etched on his face.

"Jacob?" Rachel's voice was a whisper.

The scene unfolded like a slow-motion movie. Introductions, awkward smiles, strained explanations. Jacob poured out his heart, the guilt, the regret, the news that had brought him here – his decision to finally leave the law firm, to pursue a simpler life, a life he now desperately wished he could share with her.

The silence that followed was deafening. Rachel listened, her expression unreadable. Finally, she spoke, her voice soft but firm.

"Jacob," she said, "Seeing you again brings back so many memories. But…" she turned to the man beside her, placing a hand on his arm, "This is Mark. We've built a life together, a life I cherish."

Jacob's heart plummeted. The flicker of hope that had dared to ignite extinguished with a single sentence.

Rachel continued, her voice filled with a quiet strength. "Your news is wonderful, Jacob. But you have to understand, this isn't a scene from a movie. There's no grand gesture, no running back into each other's arms. We both made choices, and we have to live with them."

There was no anger, no blame, just a deep understanding. Jacob stood there, the weight of his choices settling on him like a leaden cloak.

As he turned to leave, his voice choked with emotion, he managed a single word. "Goodbye, Rachel."

This time, the goodbye wasn't shrouded in uncertainty. It was a quiet acceptance, a bittersweet farewell to a love story that could have been, but ultimately wasn't meant to be. He walked away, not with regret, but with a newfound clarity, determined to write a new chapter in his life, a chapter filled with the lessons learned from the one he'd so carelessly closed.

Understanding Paperclipping

Paperclipping involves an ex-partner reaching out or making contact just as you've started to move on with a new relationship. The term is inspired by the recurring behaviour of Clippy, the Microsoft Office assistant, who pops up when you least need it. In the context of relationships, paperclipping can cause confusion and uncertainty, often disrupting the healing process or the stability of a new partnership.

Examples

The Elusive Texter: Weeks of silence stretch on, a communication wasteland. Then, a lone text appears on your screen - a random meme or inside joke from a past date. It's a fleeting reminder, a paperclip poking at your memory before disappearing back into the digital abyss.

The Social Media Ghost: Their profile vanishes from your dating app, leaving you wondering if you swiped left or if they simply disappeared. Then, weeks later, a familiar face pops up on your feed, "liking" a seemingly random post. Is it a sign of interest or just a digital phantom haunting your online space?

The Erratic Caller: Just when you've begun to move on, your phone rings. It's their number, a name you haven't seen in a while. You answer with a mix of curiosity and apprehension, only to be greeted by silence. The call drops, leaving you with more questions than answers. Another paperclip moment, a brief flicker of connection before vanishing into thin air.

The Birthday Pop-Up: A year of radio silence, then a notification pierces the quiet – a generic birthday wish on your social media. Was it a scheduled reminder, a programmed paperclip, or a last-minute attempt to stay relevant? The gesture feels hollow, lacking the warmth of a genuine connection.

The Unexpected Bump-In: Weeks after a fizzled connection, you find yourself at a crowded coffee shop. Across the room, a familiar face. They make eye contact, a momentary flicker of recognition followed by a quick look away. Did they see you? Did they want to be seen? The encounter is fleeting, a paperclip moment in the real world, leaving you with a lingering sense of what could have been.

The Psychology of Paperclipping

Paperclipping is driven by various psychological factors, including unresolved emotions, a desire for validation, and fear of being replaced. It often reflects the initiator's internal conflicts rather than genuine interest in rekindling the relationship.

Unresolved Emotions: The person reaching out may have unresolved feelings and a sense of unfinished business. Seeing their ex-partner move on can trigger nostalgia and a desire to reconnect.

Need for Validation: Reaching out to an ex who has moved on can be a way to seek validation. It reassures the initiator that they still matter and have an impact on their ex's life.

Fear of Replacement: Seeing an ex-partner with someone new can evoke fear of being replaced or forgotten. The initiator might reach out to reassert their presence and significance.

The Emotional Impact of Paperclipping

Paperclipping can create emotional turbulence for both the person being contacted and their new partner. It can lead to confusion, insecurity, and potential conflict in the new relationship.

Emotional Confusion: The unexpected contact from an ex can stir up old feelings and doubts, making it difficult to focus on the present relationship. It can cause emotional confusion and distraction.

Insecurity in the New Relationship: For the new partner, paperclipping can generate feelings of insecurity and jealousy. They may question the strength of their relationship and the commitment of their partner.

Potential Conflict: The presence of an ex can create tension and conflict within the new relationship. Honest communication and reassurance are essential to navigate this challenge.

Navigating Paperclipping

Dealing with paperclipping requires clear communication, firm boundaries, and a focus on the current relationship. Here are some strategies to handle this behaviour effectively.

Set Clear Boundaries: Establish and communicate clear boundaries with your ex. Let them know that while you appreciate the past, you are committed to moving forward with your new partner.

Communicate with Your Partner: Be open and honest with your current partner about the contact from your ex. Transparency builds trust and helps address any insecurities that may arise.

Focus on the Present: Concentrate on nurturing your current relationship. Invest time and effort in creating new memories and strengthening your bond with your partner.

Reflect on Intentions: Reflect on why your ex might be reaching out and what their intentions could be. This can help you approach the situation with a clear mind and prevent unnecessary emotional entanglement.

Conclusion

Paperclipping is a challenging phenomenon that can disrupt the progress of moving on and building a new relationship. By understanding the psychology behind paperclipping, recognising its emotional impact, and adopting strategies to navigate it, you can protect your emotional well-being and foster a healthy, committed relationship.

As we continue to explore the intricate dynamics of modern romance, remember to prioritise the present and future over the past. Embrace new beginnings, set firm boundaries, and communicate openly with your partner to build a foundation of trust and love.

Chapter 17

Breaking Up – Navigating the Emotional Terrain

We've traversed the complexities of the dating landscape, from situationships to ghosting, and unpacked the importance of self-respect and emotional intelligence in navigating modern love. Let us tackle a topic that evokes a difficult mix of emotions: the breakup. We'll delve into initiating a breakup with kindness, explore the emotional aftermath, and equip you with strategies to navigate this experience with grace and self-care.

Beyond the Broken Frame

The flickering candlelight cast grotesque shadows on the peeling wallpaper, a fitting backdrop for the storm brewing between Sanya and Karan. The air crackled with unspoken accusations, a stark contrast to the carefree laughter that had once filled this very room.

Four years. Four years of stolen kisses under the Eiffel Tower, whispered promises etched in the sand on a secluded Thai beach, and late-night talks that stretched into the sunrise, fueled by dreams and ambition. Now, those very dreams lay shattered on the worn wooden floorboards.

The catalyst? Karan's promotion. A dream job in London, a chance to catapult his career to dizzying heights, a chance he'd always craved. But Sanya, a budding artist on the cusp of her first solo exhibition, had roots in her hometown, roots that ran deep. Neither was willing to budge.

The conversation, when it finally erupted, was a brutal cocktail of anger and hurt. Karan, his voice laced with frustration, accused Sanya of holding him back. Sanya, eyes blazing with betrayal, countered that his ambitions had always overshadowed hers.

"It's not about holding you back," she choked out, tears blurring her vision. "It's about building a life together! Don't you get it? This isn't just about a job!"

Karan faltered, a flicker of regret crossing his face, but it was quickly replaced by a steely resolve. "We can't both have everything, Sanya. This is my chance, and I can't pass it up."

There were no tearful apologies, no desperate pleas to find a solution. The love they had built, a fortress once deemed impenetrable, had crumbled under the weight of their diverging paths. In the deafening silence that followed, a profound truth hung heavy in the air – their love story, once vibrant and full of promise, had become a cautionary tale.

Finally, Sanya stood up, her voice choked but firm. "Then go, Karan. But don't ever forget, you chose your career over us." The words hung in the air, a tombstone marking the grave of their relationship.

He left without another word, the slam of the door echoing through the empty apartment like a gunshot. The night stretched on, a tapestry woven with tears, the deafening silence punctuated by the rhythmic ticking of the clock, mocking the passage of time and the dreams that had withered and died.

The following days were a blur of exhaustion and grief. Sanya found solace in the familiar embrace of her art studio, the rhythmic strokes of her brush a cathartic release of the emotions churning within. Each painting, a canvas awash with vibrant hues and raw emotion, became a shard of their shattered past.

Slowly, with the unwavering support of her loved ones, Sanya began to piece together the fragments of her broken heart. She reconnected with old friends, their laughter a balm to her wounded soul. She poured herself into her art, her solo exhibition becoming a testament to her resilience, her raw emotions captivating a city that had watched her love story crumble.

One evening, at the bustling opening reception, amidst the clinking of glasses and vibrant chatter, Sanya saw a familiar face. Karan, his face etched with regret, stood awkwardly at the back of the room. Their eyes met briefly, a silent exchange of memories and what-ifs.

But Sanya, her eyes shining with newfound strength, simply gave him a curt nod and turned back to the crowd, her spirit unbroken. The break-up, though brutal, had been a catalyst. It had forced her to confront her vulnerabilities, to rediscover her strength, and to embrace the unknown.

The future stretched before Sanya, an uncharted territory filled with possibilities. She carried the lessons learned – the importance of communication, compromise, and the unwavering belief in her own dreams. The bad break-up, once a storm that threatened to consume her, became a turning point. It paved the way for a future filled with self-discovery, new beginnings, and the unwavering hope of finding love again, this time on her own terms, stronger and more whole than ever before.

Understanding Breakups: When Fairy Tales End

Relationships, like tapestries, are woven with threads of shared experiences and emotions. But sometimes, the colours fade, the threads fray, and the once vibrant picture loses its lustre. This is the essence of a breakup. It's a recognition that a relationship has run its course, and a difficult decision to move forward on separate paths.

Examples

The Phone Call Conversation: The silence stretches, heavy and thick. One trembling hand reaches for the phone, the other hovering over a familiar number. A deep breath, a dial tone, and then a voice, once filled with warmth, now laced with a formality that chills. Words are exchanged, hesitant at first, then flowing in a torrent of explanations and apologies. Finally, a heavy sigh, a choked "goodbye," and the click that severs the connection. The phone rests on the table, a silent witness to the end of a love story.

The Unsent Text: Fingers fly across the screen, pouring out a heart overflowing with emotions – hurt, anger, love, and a desperate plea for reconciliation. But with each reread, the words feel hollow, unable to bridge the chasm that has grown between them. A single tear falls, blurring the screen. With a heavy heart, the message is deleted, a silent goodbye echoing in the emptiness of the unsent text.

The Deleted Photos: Memories scroll by, each one a snapshot of a shared moment, a stolen glance, a whispered promise. A bittersweet smile plays on lips as fingers linger over a particularly cherished image. But with a final tap, it joins the others in the digital graveyard, a deliberate act of letting go. The screen remains dark, a blank canvas for new beginnings.

The Unfriended Profile: Once a source of joy, the social media feed now feels like a battlefield of shared memories. Happy pictures and inside jokes become painful reminders of what's lost. With a final click, the unfriend button is pressed, a digital curtain drawn on a chapter that's closed. The silence is deafening, but also strangely liberating.

The Empty Room: Boxes line the walls, remnants of a life once shared. The air hangs heavy with unspoken words and the lingering scent of a familiar perfume. Footsteps echo on the bare floor as the last box is carried out, the door closed with a soft click. The room stands empty, a stark canvas waiting to be filled with new memories, a future yet unwritten.

Reasons for Breakups: When Paths Diverge

Every relationship ends for unique reasons, but some common themes emerge:

Loss of Compatibility: People evolve. Values, goals, or life aspirations might shift, leaving you feeling increasingly incompatible with your partner.

Communication Breakdown: Without open and honest communication, misunderstandings fester, and emotional connection weakens. Unresolved conflicts can signal the need for a change of course.

Unmet Needs: Relationships thrive when needs are met. If a relationship consistently fails to fulfil your emotional or physical needs, resentment can build, leading to a difficult decision.

External Factors: Job changes, long-distance moves, a new love interest or even family pressures can create immense stress on a relationship, making it difficult to sustain.

The Dreaded Conversation: Initiating a Breakup with Kindness

While breakups are rarely easy, approaching them with honesty and empathy can ease the pain for both parties. Here are some tips for initiating a respectful conversation:

1. **Choose the Right Time and Place**: Don't initiate a breakup in a public place or over text. Find a private, quiet space where you can have a face-to-face conversation.

2. **Be Direct and Honest:** Avoid sugarcoating the truth or making false promises. Explain your reasons for wanting to break up in a clear and honest way.

3. **Validate Their Feelings:** Acknowledge your partner's pain and express empathy for their emotional state. Let them know their feelings are valid.

4. **Focus on "I" Statements:** Instead of accusatory language, use "I" statements to explain how the relationship has impacted

you. "I feel like we've grown apart" is more constructive than "You're never there for me."

5. **Set Boundaries:** After the conversation, establish clear boundaries regarding communication and contact. Let your partner know what level of interaction you're comfortable with moving forward.

Examples of Breakup Conversations:

1. **Scenario:** You've been dating someone for several months, but you don't see a long-term future together.

   Conversation: "I've enjoyed getting to know you, but I've been thinking a lot lately, and I don't feel like we're on the same page about what we want in a relationship. I'm looking for something more serious, and I don't think we're a good fit long-term. I understand this might be disappointing, and I truly value the time we've spent together."

2. **Scenario:** You've been in a long-term relationship, but communication has broken down, and resentment has built up.

   Conversation: "We've been together for a long time, and lately, things haven't felt right. I feel like we're constantly arguing, and we don't seem to connect anymore. I care about you, but I don't think we can be happy together if things don't change. Perhaps some time apart would be helpful to reflect on what we both want."

Picking Up the Pieces: Healing After a Breakup

Breakups are emotionally charged events. You might experience a range of feelings, including sadness, anger, confusion, and loneliness. Here are some strategies for navigating the emotional aftermath:

Allow Yourself to Feel: Don't suppress your emotions. Acknowledge your pain and give yourself time to grieve the end of the relationship.

Seek Support: Lean on your friends, family, or a therapist for emotional support during this difficult time. Talking about your feelings can be incredibly cathartic.

Practice Self-Care: Prioritise your physical and mental well-being. Engage in activities you enjoy, eat healthy foods, exercise and get enough sleep. Self-care is essential for emotional healing.

Focus on Self-Discovery: This is an opportunity for personal growth. Reflect on what you learned from the relationship and what you want in a future partner. Journaling, spending time in nature, or pursuing hobbies can be helpful tools for self-discovery.

Embrace New Beginnings: The end of a relationship doesn't diminish your worth or your ability to find love again. See this as an opportunity for new experiences and a chance to find a love that truly resonates with your heart.

Conclusion: Moving Forward with an Open Heart

Love adventurers, breakups are an inevitable part of life's journey. They can be painful, but they also offer an opportunity for growth and self-discovery. Remember, the end of a relationship doesn't define you. Here are some key takeaways to carry with you:

Prioritise Self-Respect: Don't let a breakup define your worth. Maintain your self-worth and remember that you deserve a fulfilling relationship.

Learn from the Past: Reflect on your past relationship and identify areas for personal growth. This knowledge will help you make healthier choices in the future.

Embrace New Beginnings: The end of a relationship isn't the end of your love story. See this as an opportunity for new experiences and a chance to find love that truly resonates with your heart.

So, dear adventurers, remember that love is a continuous journey. Keep your heart open to the possibilities that lie ahead. The world is full of beautiful connections waiting to be discovered. May your future be filled with love, laughter, and meaningful connections.

Chapter 18

Game Over – Ditching the Drama and Embracing Real Love

Love adventurers, congratulations! You've reached the final chapter of our crash course in Love Games - decoding modern romance. We've tackled everything from situationships that fizzle faster than a damp firework to the not-so-subtle art of the bread crumbing. We've learned to sidestep the drama of ghosting and dodge the emotional curveballs of orbiting. Now, let's talk about ditching the game-playing altogether and embracing genuine connection.

Love Shouldn't Feel Like Dodgeball:

Because seriously, who enjoys getting smacked in the face with a red rubber ball (or a mixed message text)? Love is about building something real, not participating in a high school gym class reject. Imagine cuddling on the couch with someone who throws emotional curve balls instead of popcorn. No thanks!

Authenticity is the New Black (and Every Other Color):

Ditch the filters, the carefully crafted online personas, and the pressure to be someone you're not. The right person will love you for your weird laugh, your questionable dance moves, and your undying love for that embarrassing childhood band. Own your quirks, celebrate your individuality, and let your true flag fly. Think of yourself as a walking, talking meme – the right person will find you hilarious, relatable, and endlessly entertaining (in a good way, of course).

Communication: It's Not Just for Astronauts (or Couples' Therapists):

Yes, talking can be scary, but it's the cornerstone of healthy relationships. Express your needs, wants, and anxieties openly and honestly. Listen actively to your partner, and ditch the passive-aggressive mind games. Because let's be honest, nobody has time to decipher cryptic texts or play detective for signs of affection. Imagine trying to crack the Da Vinci Code just to figure out if someone likes you. Exhausting!

Let's Make Love Fun Again!

Remember that spark that ignited your love story in the first place? Don't let it get lost in a sea of routine and unspoken expectations. Flirt, have spontaneous adventures, and laugh together until your sides hurt. Life's too short for boring relationships, so keep the spark alive and don't be afraid to be playful and lighthearted. Think of yourselves as two goofy penguins on a date – waddling around, clumsy but cute, and having a blast together.

So ditch the dating playbooks, adventurers! Throw out the rulebooks on how love is "supposed" to happen. Embrace your authentic self, cultivate open communication, and prioritise genuine connection. Because at the end of the day, love isn't a game; it's a beautiful, messy, and utterly extraordinary adventure.

Now get out there, explore the world of connections, and write your own epic love story!

But wait, there's more! This journey of love isn't a one-shot deal. It's a continuous exploration, filled with unexpected twists and turns. Remember, even the most epic love stories have their fair share of awkward moments, silly arguments, and the occasional fight over who gets the last slice of pizza. But as long as you approach your relationship with honesty, humour, and a whole lot of heart, you'll be well on your way to happily ever after (or at least a pretty darn good happily for now). So grab your metaphorical compass, set your course for love, and remember, dear adventurers, the greatest love story is the one you write together.

As we close the book on our journey through the love games, let us carry with us the lessons learned, the memories cherished, and the hope for a brighter tomorrow. In the labyrinth of modern romance, where love and heartbreak intertwine, one thing remains certain: the journey of love is as intricate as it is beautiful. So, dear reader, embrace the complexities of love with open arms, knowing that within its depths lie endless possibilities for growth, connection, and fulfilment.

For in the end, it is not the games we play but the love we share that defines us – a love that transcends boundaries, defies expectations, and endures through the ages. And so, with a twinkle in our eyes and a skip in our step, let us embark on our next great adventure: the quest for true love in all its messy, unpredictable glory.

Love is not a game to be won or lost but a journey to be cherished and embraced.